EXPERIMENTAL COLLEGES

Their Role in American Higher Education

PRICE: $3.50

EXPERIMENTAL COLLEGES

Their Role in American Higher Education

Edited by W. HUGH STICKLER
PROFESSOR OF HIGHER EDUCATION
FLORIDA STATE UNIVERSITY

FLORIDA STATE UNIVERSITY

TALLAHASSEE, 1964

Printed and bound in the United States of America
by the Douglas Printing Company, Inc.

DEDICATION

Dr. Gordon W. Blackwell throughout his presidency at the Florida State University has shown a consistent concern for the highest standards of scholarship blended with a personal regard for each student as an individual. Perhaps nowhere else have these concerns been more evident than in the events leading to the Wakulla Springs Colloquium on Experimental Colleges and in the plans for a student-oriented experimental college at Florida State. This book is dedicated to him in gratitude for his vision and support of the best in undergraduate education.

FOREWORD

W E in higher education need most of all the time to think, evaluate, and plan. For there is the necessary, yet dangerous, involvement in the day-to-day and week-to-week problems created by rapid growth, inadequate funds, and lack of understanding among our constituents. We spend our time putting out brush fires, while doing little or nothing to prevent a potential wide-spread fire which threatens the large, complex universities.

I refer to the threat to quality undergraduate education. This, I believe, is the most urgent and most universal problem facing universities today.

This threat derives from several sources: rapid growth with its attendant problem of numbers; increasing emphasis, even though needed and proper, upon advanced graduate education and the research role of the university especially in the sciences; employment of new devices which impersonalize the teaching process; extra-curricular activities unrelated to and often in conflict with primary educational functions. These factors have tended to weaken the effectiveness of undergraduate education in the American university.

We at Florida State have determined to do something about this threat. Hence the conference here reported; hence also our own proposal for a different type of residential undergraduate college in a relatively large, complex university setting. The problem which has motivated us is widespread and critical.

We are indebted to the conference participants for exciting days of stimulating discussion. American universities must develop new approaches to undergraduate education. We hope that this volume will suggest some of the paths ahead.

GORDON W. BLACKWELL, *President*
Florida State University
Tallahassee, Florida

v

EﾍRLY in the academic year 1963-1964 President Gordon W. Blackwell appointed a Committee on an Experimental College* to consider problems of undergraduate education in large universities in general and in the Florida State University in particular. The Committee met frequently—usually once a week. On many occasions, because of his manifest interest, President Blackwell met with the group.

The Committee had met only a few times when it came to two conclusions:

a. All is not well in undergraduate education in large American universities, including the Florida State University. There must be a better way—or better ways—of providing meaningful education at this level.

b. A carefully planned and creatively operated experimental college holds considerable promise—or at least the possibility—of providing better undergraduate education in our institution. The Committee recommends the establishment of a pilot or prototype college in the Florida State University. If it succeeds as anticipated, such an experimental college may prove to be the first of a series of small colleges on this campus within which much—or possibly all—of the undergraduate program of this University will later be accomplished.

Once the decision had been made to recommend the establishment of a prototype college as an integral part of the Florida State University, the Committee felt a need to know much more about experimental programs in other institutions of higher education before recommending the broad outlines for the pilot college on its own campus. This felt need led to a "Colloquium on Experimental Colleges" which was held at Wakulla Springs, 15 miles south of Tallahassee, Florida, in the spring of 1964.

No claim is made that the Colloquium was comprehensive

---

*Members of the Committee on an Experimental College included: R. R. Oglesby, Dean of Students (Chairman); E. Laurence Chalmers, Jr., Assistant Dean of the Faculties; John K. Folger, Dean of the Graduate School; J. Paul Reynolds, Dean of the College of Arts and Sciences; N. Orwin Rush, Director of Libraries; Louis Shores, Dean of the Library School; and W. Hugh Stickler, Head of the Department of Higher Education.

or that it included all or even a large proportion of the experimental colleges currently operating in the United States. Rather the Committee arbitrarily selected for participation in the conference institutions: (a) which it felt were representative of experimental colleges in general, (b) which might profitably be considered in a forum on experimental colleges and their place in American higher education, and (c) which might prove helpful to the Committee as it moved forward in its preliminary planning for the prototype experimental college on the Florida State University campus. The Committee has been pleased with its choices of institutions. Insofar as the Committee is concerned, the Colloquium accomplished in full measure the purposes for which it was operated.

The volume which follows is not a record of the conference proceedings, but it is an outgrowth of the Colloquium. The first chapter is essentially the keynote address presented by Dr. Marjorie Carpenter at the opening session. Some of the next eleven chapters were written before the Colloquium, some were completed during the conference, and some were written after the Colloquium; none, however, was read at the conference itself. Rather the contents were discussed informally in each instance with full knowledge on the part of each contributor that a chapter concerning his institution would later become a part of this book. The final chapter by Dr. B. Lamar Johnson is basically his summary and critique of the Colloquium presented at the closing session.

The Florida State University Committee on an Experimental College and the present editor who functions in behalf of that Committee are indebted to many agencies and persons for assistance in operating the Colloquium on Experimental Colleges and in preparing the manuscript for this volume.

The Southern Regional Education Board helped in three ways: (1) together with the Florida State University it sponsored the Wakulla Springs Colloquium; (2) several SREB representatives participated in the conference; and (3) it assisted the University by contributing funds toward both the operation of the Colloquium and the publication of this book. The American Council on Education, the Association of College and Research Libraries, the Board of Control of the State University System of Florida, the Danforth Foundation, the Ford Foundation, and the Southern Association of Colleges and Schools also sent representatives to the Colloquium. To all of these agencies go thanks for assistance in this total undertaking.

Special thanks go to President Gordon W. Blackwell of the Florida State University. Without his unfailing interest, support, and encouragement neither the Colloquium nor this book would have become a reality. Appreciation is also expressed to the authors of the respective chapters which together comprise this volume. Altogether some fifty or sixty persons participated in the Colloquium; their penetrating discussions undoubtedly sharpened the content of many of the chapters which follow. Gratitude goes to each of these individuals for taking time from his busy schedule to participate in this significant undertaking. Lastly indebtedness to Mrs. Jeanne Z. Bevis, Executive Secretary in the Department of Higher Education at the Florida State University, is gratefully acknowledged for preparing the final typescript.

W. HUGH STICKLER, *Editor*

Florida State University
Tallahassee, Florida

TABLE OF CONTENTS

Chapter 1

THE ROLE OF EXPERIMENTAL COLLEGES IN AMERICAN HIGHER EDUCATION

By Marjorie Carpenter*

The first part of the title or topic assigned me has a literal meaning of real significance. The word "role" means a part assigned an actor in a play. Are we, then, considering the part assigned the experimental college in a drama to be played out on the American stage? Play acting connotes a certain unreality. The use of this word may, in fact, point up something which *has* been happening. Let me use an analogy (always dangerous in its limitations). In considering the visual arts, it is clear that many people prefer merely a surface likeness, a painting whose lines, colors, and shapes are comfortingly like familiar objects. Many so-called artists have great facility in such representational pictures. But when the creative artist feels and tries to express what is underneath the surface, he performs a different and more significant service for all of us. According to Leonard Bernstein in his discussion of Beethoven the great composer "magnifies the essence." A photographer can capture the outer appearance; the genius helps us enter into his perception until our understanding of ourselves and the world is enriched immeasurably.

I should like to think that in higher education we are not play acting—not just copying the generally recognized image of a process called education, which etymologically suggests that "we lead students out" from their narrow concepts of themselves and their world. I should like to think that we try to capture the very essence of that valuable experience.

Consider the phrase "experimental college." Very simply this

---

*Miss Carpenter is Chairman of the Division of Humanities, Stephens College, Columbia, Missouri.

is an educational institution which is trying to be a college.
Literally a college is a community, a group of people. From
this point on, there will be varying ideas about what the community is trying to do. I should like to think that they are in
pursuit of something more than surface phenomena, something more than imitation of other institutions. In trying to be
a college, they have to ponder all of the factors which make this
"collegium" an especially valuable part of the larger needs of
their clientele, a very special set of human beings alive in
America today—and that has to mean in the world today. This
will necessarily involve "experimenting." To capture the essence, one must experiment with his medium in order to magnify, to spotlight, to throw into effective juxtaposition the
essential elements which will make the desired total impact.
This is no static effort either on the part of the institution
which we call a college nor on the part of the faculty member
who adventures with students beyond and beneath the surface.

Yet we all know that the great majority of colleges copy recognized educational institutions. They may copy very good elements with great facility. This we accept; we do not expect
every composer, every painter to be a genius; but we should, as
critics of education (do I dare say, as leaders?) recognize the
copy for which it is; we should see the point beyond which
copying is dangerous; we should understand the need in certain periods of educational history for a Renaissance which
makes an effort to capture the new spirit in the air: we should
be able to spot the assumptions which have become outworn.

There is, perhaps, no need to belabor the fact that most universities and colleges copy the prestige institutions. An amaz-
ing example was the occasion of the publication of Harvard's
volume on *General Education in a Free Society*. Institutions
which had been laboring to attain a sound general education
program and good general education courses were some of
them annoyed and some of them pleased to receive the stamp
of respectability from the well-established institution. The nod
of approval gave a certain sense of security. The term "general
education" ceased to be a debutante and became one of the
"four hundred." At this very point, dangers became apparent;
vitality and freshness began to languish; blind imitation be-

came common, along with a mouthing of words, symptomatic of surface adaptations with no real change in "the essence."

It is easy to become cynical about such climbing on the bandwagon. Actually, in all honesty, one has to admit that a certain amount of good accrued: some faculty members began to realize that they could learn something in a new area even though they had a degree in a different field. Healthful doubts were raised about the degree of over departmentalization and over specialization which we had been copying from German graduate schools. A new focus on student as well as subject matter began, with trial balloons in counseling and attempts to assist students in bringing into significant focus the inter-relationships of various courses.

Americans are very prone to swing from one end of the pendulum to the other. It may be helpful in evaluating this phenomenon to consider the warnings of William Sheldon in his book, *The Promethean and Epimethean Conflict*. He says that the prophet, or visionary person, who brings the fire of inspiration from Heaven, as Prometheus did, lives in each of us. This spirit lives alongside an Epimetheus who symbolizes the priest, the consolidator. At his peril, according to Sheldon who is both medical doctor and psychiatrist, does the individual turn away permanently from either. It is fatal to say at one point, "I am getting nowhere with this routine; what I need to do is to become a prophet, to let the world know my vision; and this is *all* that matters." If he does this, the vision becomes clouded and empty and irrelevant to life. On the other hand, it is equally dangerous to reject the prophetic vision and settle for routine consolidation which rapidly becomes more arid and increasingly more of a routine without freshness and without vitality. The psychiatrist has seen what this does to the individual who suffers what he calls a "dying back of the mind." We must, he claims, keep the two impulses in solution; laugh at ourselves when they come in conflict; but at our peril seek to resolve this kind of conflict.

Our institutions suffer, Sheldon points out, from the lack of understanding of these same principles. For example, the church hears restatements of theology based on relevance to new insights about man's relationship to spiritual truths; and what happens? The conservatives are shocked and they jump up and down in the same place saying, "We shall have none of this." Then the corner of truth which could have illumined the thinking of all of us is seized by charlatans to form the basis of a new sect. You need no chart to point up the frequency with which this has happened in education. The label "progressive education" has been stamped on some rather peculiar models which are quite at variance with the tenets of John Dewey.

The millennium will be reached in the development of experimental and experimenting colleges when new ideas are welcomed by administration and faculty without defensiveness about established tradition and with recognition of the need to try a suggested new approach and evaluate it before it is rejected. The crisis becomes clear when, on the one hand, the consolidator finds the vision only partially helpful; and the visionary, on the other hand, is forced to see his idea in the total setting. Vision is, after all, usually the contribution of one or a few; the consolidators are many. There is a very great temptation for Epimetheus to reject after only one trial; and it is a natural reaction for Prometheus to sulk if any part of his bright idea is brought into question. An equally serious pitfall is the tendency to settle for an inadequate compromise which loses the real spark of the initial inspiration.

Let us suppose that we have been able to recognize copies for what they are; let us say that we do understand the point at which imitation is dangerous and stupid and when it is helpful. Let us even be sufficiently optimistic to assume that we can deftly transfer a brand new concept from the mind of a teacher or a dean or a president on to the worktable where willing faculty members enthusiastically try it out. There remains another task confronting us if we are to understand the role of the experimental college in American education today. Do we recognize that there is a special need for a Renaissance in higher education today? A corollary question has to be asked: do we recognize the assumptions which are obstacles to a new look at a radically different world?

To say that change is in the air is an understatement. Margaret Mead has said that no change is so great as the change in the rate of change. Ever since sputnik went into orbit, we have whirled from one new phenomenon to another. Let us think of just three. First, we have seen automation advance to a point where it is welcomed as a relief from drudgery and at the same time feared because of its creation of problems of unemployment. Second, we have seen atomic energy develop to a point where we are uncertain whether to greet with enthusiasm the new possibilities it has created as a supplement to our depleted resources or whether to recoil with horror at its obvious potentials for total destruction. Third, we have seen communication and transportation develop with a speed which makes any lingering hope of isolation impossible. With corresponding haste new nations emerge with demands which clamor for attention. We are, in fact, so aware of change and insecurity that mental instability on a large scale is the result. It is not surprising that these stimuli leave us uncertain and confused. It *is* surprising that we do not see immediate implications for education in each of the new developments just mentioned.

If automation creates unemployment, listen to the conclusions of three experts in economics. These men were heard by Stephens College students over our amplified telephone course in "Great Issues in Contemporary Society." A. H. Raskin, the *New York Times* expert on labor unions, said that young people must stay in school, or even go back to school, to learn more than one skill. He also underlined the need for highly educated and imaginative leaders of labor unions. Carey Williams, the distinguished editor of *The Nation,* concluded his talk on automation with a challenge for students and faculty in our colleges to direct their energies to other important aspects of life than the kind of labor which machines can do better. He says:

> Automation is basically not an economic problem nor a governmental problem; it is one which stems from our social ethic. We must embrace a new kind of ethic which includes leisure pursuits, social service, something which benefits society. We must decide what values to encourage and what we want human beings to become . . . We must motivate people to be educated for self fulfillment; we must create meaningful values if life is to have meaning . . . Automation removes labor, drudgery. Work is the kind of thing we do in

self-fulfillment because it is important to us: creative work for example—books, pictures, art.

Finally, Adolf Berle, the exponent of free enterprise and its responsibilities, summed up his comments by saying:

Man is a prisoner unless he is a participant in society. It is sometimes said that we shall not need as much work. My own feeling is that what we need is a greater consciousness of the work which needs to be done. Take a single value, the value of beauty for example. If the community wanted a beautiful city it would have it; but it would have to work enormously to get it . . . It is silly to say that we are doing everything which needs to be done—we need only stroll around town to know that this is not so . . . If there seems to be less work needed, it means that we are not culturally advanced far enough or are not sensitive enough to insist that work be done . . . The ultimate arbiter of planning for the future is not going to be the economist; it will be that sector of the community which understands and guards the values: the great value of truth as we see it in science, the real value of beauty which covers all from the representational arts to architecture, the great value of education which leads to the beauty of the community and the employment which goes with it.

Do these conclusions about a radically new day brought on by automation and an increased sensitivity to the arts find a response in our colleges? Do we do more than hand on to students "our cultural heritage"? Do we encourage them to discover new satisfactions, new self-fulfillment in creating and performing in the arts? Do we consider the need for suggesting ways of taking leadership for starting local councils on the arts? Do we perceive the necessity for a citizenry which is aesthetically literate, aware of present ugliness and potential beauty in the various communities of the country?

The answer to this first challenge of the new day is that we are timidly doing something in isolated cases.

What about the vast increase in scientific knowledge in this nuclear age? The multiplication of science courses, better teaching of mathematics, and even earlier presentation of new scientific knowledge than we had thought possible—all of these developments have pointed up our awareness of a new day in which the average citizen feels himself an inhabitant in space and a terrified participant in control of nuclear energy. Do we, at the same time, perceive that what Margaret Mead calls "a lateral transmission of knowledge" may well be the flexible answer to pressures for more and more scientific courses? As she points out, it is not a question of the expert teacher demonstrating new facts to the younger generation, but rather a "sharing of knowledge by the informed with the uninformed, whatever their ages." Or do we consider education commensurate with degrees and a certain number of credit hours obtained in residence in a recognized college for a definite number of years—and, we might add, in classes of a special size which meet for a specified number of minutes? If the latter is true can we possibly face the implications of education for extremely rapid adaptation to a new age, remembering as Mead says, that "no one will live all of his life in the world to which he was born, and no one will die in the world in which he worked in his maturity."

The last in my sampling of evidences of a brand new day is the increasing importance of the number of new nations which are, whether we like it or not, inevitably a part of our immediate world. In response to this new development there have been timid feelers and partial answers on the part of our colleges. More foreign students are on our campuses; more of our students spend a year abroad under the aegis of their home colleges; more courses in social science take into account new and broad concepts of today's world and peoples. More institutions are using lecturers and materials on topics other than those dictated by the western world. It is even true that some flexibility occurs in giving credit to educational experience obtained abroad even when it was not directed by the degree granting institution. But our vision is still too limited for the huge canvas which provides today's backdrop.

If, then, we know that change is in the air, if we recognize the temptation to be merely imitative even in the presence of a Renaissance whose complete newness outshines all previous eras, what must we do? What are the blocks to moving forward with speed and zest? Einstein accounted for his accomplishments by saying he "merely challenged the axioms." Let me mention only two of the many assumptions about higher education which go unchallenged.

1. The first unchallenged assumption is this: *the major responsibility of a college is to young people just out of high school.* We might ask: is our timing all wrong? A superintendent of education for the Province of Ontario said years ago: "At present we are throwing pearls before swine while Rome burns." In this delightfully mixed metaphor there is a disturbing question which we rarely consider (except perhaps in adult education courses). Do we really know when to release active young people for action and when to capitalize on mature experience for discussions of philosophy and economics?

Pursue this still further. Do we honestly believe the truth which we mouth? "Education is never finished; continuing education is the important emphasis of the day." If we perceive truth here, what do the private colleges do about recruitment of students, about provision for admission of non-high school graduates, about flexible arrangements for the education of mature women? Is there an experimental college whose entire plan is free from time limits and age limits?

2. The second unchallenged assumption is this: *we must have grades and total credits for a degree in order to identify the college graduate.* Should we even talk about a college graduate? If we perceive that the assignment of grades is playing into the hands of the American competitive system with its demand and pressures for success, then why do we insist on having symbols which registrars pass from institution to institution? Even Goddard College and Sarah Lawrence College face the transfer demand for grades.

For that matter, if we feel that we should try to offset the race for status symbols in our society, should we not abolish the status symbols of faculty rank? Furthermore, if we underline the need for a degree as a mark of the completion of a college education, does this really educate the student?

There are many more unexamined assumptions, and they do block progress. What, then, are the keys to wise experimentation? What *is* the contribution which the experimental college can make to American education today? May I also add that there is an inconceivable contribution to be made. I also think the hurdles can seem almost insurmountable if the experimental college undertakes a completely new look at today's needs in higher education. At this point I should like to make what seems to be a digression, and it certainly is another use of the dangerous method of analogy. Let me insist that I am not preaching a post-Easter sermon when I quote Paul Tillich; but I should like to borrow some insights which this contemporary philosopher seems to have when he considers our national scene.

The final chapter in his book, *The Shaking of the Foundations,* Tillich entitles "I Am Doing a New Thing." He begins with a passage from Isaiah (43:18-19): "Remember not the former things, neither consider the things of old. Behold, I am doing a new thing; even now it is springing to light. Do you not perceive it?" He proceeds with other quotations repeating this emphasis on newness. Most applicable to our considerations today is the parable from Matthew (9:16-17): "No one puts a piece of new cloth on an old garment, for the patch tears away from the garment, and a worse tear is made. Neither is new wine put into old wineskins; if it is, the skins burst and the wine is spilled, and the skins are destroyed; but new wine is put into new wineskins, and so both are preserved."

Tillich, then, calls attention to the fact that all of the Biblical texts which comment on the old and the new use those terms in ways which must be defined and understood. The prophets do not call for the new because they consider the new better or because it comes later; nor do they fail to recognize that there is one kind of old which does not age. They mean by "old" that which passes away and shall not be remembered. Growth is recognized as "gain and loss at the same time."

Let me quote Tillich's exact words:

Periods of history which are determined by one idea suppress the truth of other possible ideas. Every decision excludes possibilities and makes life narrower. Youth is openness. But every decision closes doors. And that cannot be avoided; it is an inescapable destiny. . . . The law of growth lends us greatness, and therefore tragedy. For the excluded possibilities belong to us; and they have a right of their own. Therefore, they take vengeance on our lives which have excluded them. They may die; and with them, great powers of life and large resources of creativity. For life, as it grows, becomes a restricted power, more rigid and inflexible, less able to adjust itself to new situations and new demands. Or, on the other hand, the excluded possibilities may *not* die. They may remain within us, repressed, hidden, and dangerous, prepared to break into the life process, not as a creative resource, but as a destructive disease. . . . Self-limitations and self-destruction—both carry death.

Extend these principles historically and very briefly look at some historical examples:

We decided for freedom and excluded the security, social and spiritual, without which man cannot grow.

We decided for means to control nature and society; we have excluded ends.

We have decided for a secular world; we have excluded the deep things for which religion stands.

Tillich then concludes:

It is not the old which creates the new. That which creates the new is beyond the old and beyond the new. We must not continue to say, "We know where the new will come from— it will come from *this* institution, or *this* movement, or *this* philosophy." None of these, of course, is excluded from being the place where the new will appear. But none of these guarantees its appearance. . . . We must realize as profoundly as possible that the former things have become old, that they destroy our period just when we try most courageously to preserve the best of it. . . . In no way but the most passionate striving for the new shall we become aware that the old is old and dying. . . . A new which is not able to throw the old into the past, in remembrance as well as in reality, is not the really new.

As I read of experimental colleges which have tried very hard to have new wineskins into which they pour their new wine, it seems to me that they suffer from a lack of profound conviction that "the old is old and dying." Granted, it is an almost insurmountable hurdle to "throw the old into the past in remembrance as well as in reality." For example, the old garment made from credit hours, regularly scheduled courses, institutional campuses, courses which will transfer, catalogue listings of offerings, and goals which smack of staleness so much that we hesitate even to mouth the stated objectives—all of these surface marks of the traditional college are "very much held in remembrance" as new patches are sewn on. Perhaps we can see this best in the case of the catalogue statement of objectives. A passion adequate enough to inspire the new today would automatically erase even the tape on which are recorded such phrases as:

> We offer the student a well rounded liberal arts education.
> We aim to educate good citizens.
> We develop the talents of each individual.
> In a democratic society this college seeks both freedom and responsibility for its students.
> It is possible for the student to take highly specialized courses and still obtain a broad educational base.
> We educate our students in their cultural heritage and at the same time prepare them for the future.

Is the clue, then, to a genuinely experimental college a faculty which can be fired with the idea of "passionately striving for the new"? If this passion is strong enough, will the all-too-widely felt faculty resistance to change be overcome: for example, the instructor who insists on his graduate concept of what can be expected from a college freshman, the specialist who sees the importance of his department with trade union fervor, the traditionalist who insists that Latin grammar is essential for an adequate use of the English language, the professor who waves the standard of academic excellence when he means piling on work and failing a large percentage of students? You could increase the list immeasurably.

Is the key for the administration, now pathetically bogged down with financial worries, a shift to this same "passionate striving for the new"? Certainly the disorientation which any institution must face when it tries to blot out all remembrance of past goals is tremendous. There are always alumni who remember the "good old days" as well as faculty members with vested interest in the once new project, now old. Even the newly created colleges run into a diluting of the original passionate conviction with every new addition to the faculty and with the registration of every student whose parents expect just what our tradition in this country has conditioned them to expect: success in a material sense.

Is it true, then, that the experiments with new ingredients for the new wineskins are all doomed to failure? My answer would be "Yes" *if* we insist on our belief that the new will come in any special way. However, there are possibly some emphases which will guide us toward improvement: recognition of the need for counseling and for integrated courses which cut across departmental lines, careful concern for the learning which goes on in dormitories, more attention to continuing education, more diversified ways of arranging schedules, more variety in the approach to learning, stimulation of the faculty to prepare new materials for teaching, increase in world travel, recognition of many approaches to learning other than the traditional academic approach, information about new devices for teaching and learning, and above all study of the clientele of those who come for an education and of the personnel who will serve them. Yet, any one of these suggestions for improvement can be self-defeating if we insist that any *one* is *the* answer. We may simply become bogged down and inflexible; we may lose the "passionate striving for the new." Then the consolidators will win; the charlatan will run off with the new idea and adapt it to some lesser and more remunerative purpose of his own.

Let us not, then, concentrate on patches: the superimposition of programs of independent thinking, honors programs, and similar devices. Suppose, rather, that we return to Tillich for his statement of the one essential: "That which creates the new is beyond the old and beyond the new—it comes at the moment when we have lost hope of ever finding it. . . . A thing is new, really new, in the degree to which it is eternal. . . . Love is the power of the new in every man and in all history: it cannot age."

This statement is borne out by research psychologists. It has direct implications for us. Can we perceive its relation to the process of creating an experimental college? If this unaging force of love is accepted for the power it is, we get at once a different attitude towards recalcitrant faculty members—even towards overly conservative administrative officials. What is more important, it follows immediately that students as individuals and also as the special group for the special college are of central importance in every decision. Does subject matter cease to be important? Of course not. The kind of subject matter, the type of learning experience will be planned with "passionate care." But certain things will not be included simply because they always have been nor because the instructors find them easier to present. New relationships between courses will be developed not as a "gimmick" to demonstrate that one is experimenting with a different kind of curriculum, but because organically this sequence, this combination has a logical continuity for this special student, this special group. Only *for the time* can this be considered true. The new will become old and out-worn. Flexibility must go hand in hand with the love and concern; research must be intertwined inextricably with any new development unless staleness and decay are to develop.

Therefore, next to warm concern for those we teach, I would put constant research as the contribution of the experimental college which can say proudly: "Behold, I do a new thing." A questing spirit is one important touchstone. The passionate desire to create what is adequate for today's student results inevitably in a restless questing spirit. Sometime ago an artist told me that you can separate the significant artists from the poor ones by the steady pressure on new use of media, new combinations of elements. But this can be arid experimentation unless there is a desire to communicate something of significance. Research for self aggrandizement on the part of a faculty member does not "magnify the essence" for a student. It is none the less true that the pressure to communicate more adequately next time is a driving force for the greatest artists and the greatest teachers. Frank Lloyd Wright, when asked what he considered his most successful building, said to Hugh Downs: "Why, the next one, my dear boy, the next one."

The questing spirit, the restless insistence that the way is going to break for a Renaissance in higher education, the kind of passionate intensity that this be achieved—this attitude has to be rooted in a love of people, students and faculty. It has to be accompanied by tolerance for the seemingly incompatible consolidator; but the vision must not be lost even though only a handful of people are willing to face the pain of creating a genuinely experimental college.

The challenge today is trumpeted so loud that we must heed. If we turn coward before the great obstacles and fail to fight, those of us who are faint hearted may hear the taunt of the courageous. In the words of Henry IV to the dilatory Crillon we shall hear: "Hang yourself, brave Crillon; we fought at Arques and you were not there." How much better to hear it echoed: "Behold, you have created a new thing." Then the experimental college will have found its role and made its contribution to higher education in days of real Renaissance.

Chapter 2

ANTIOCH COLLEGE AS AN EXPERIMENTAL INSTITUTION

By Esther A. Oldt*

External observers often find Antioch College a puzzle and a paradox on American higher education. How, skeptics ask, can students who spend half their time working on jobs often unrelated to their major studies achieve top academic standing? How can such a time-consuming plan include both general arts and sciences and an adequate grounding in a professional field? Surely the work program results in vocationalism or in superficiality rather than thorough scholarship.

Yet only thirty years after Antioch's work-study plan began, a number of studies showed Antioch to be one of the top ten colleges in the country in the production of young scholars and scientists. Antioch was one of only eight institutions in the United States with highest scholastic indices in all three areas: sciences, social sciences, and humanities. Achievement scores of Antioch graduates in the area tests of the Graduate Record Examinations placed them among the top five of all colleges using the GRE tests.

In 1961 George Stern of Syracuse University found Reed, Antioch, Swarthmore, and Oberlin heading a list of 67 colleges he studied and rated for high intellectual climate.[1] A five-year study made by the Center for the Study of Higher Education

*Miss Oldt is Research Associate, Antioch Education Abroad, Antioch College, Yellow Springs, Ohio.

[1]For studies mentioned and others along similar lines see:

Alexander W. Astin, " 'Productivity' of Undergraduate Institutions," *Science*, Vol. 140, 13 April 1962.

Alexander W. Astin, "Undergraduate Institutions and the Production of Scientists," *Science*, Vol. 141, 26 July 1963.

Report of David Johnson, Luther College, Decorah, Iowa, "Doctorates Earned by Graduates of Liberal Arts Colleges." (Evidently unpublished.)

of the University of California at Berkeley, when results are published, in 1965, will carry further evidence of intellectual and scholastic attainments at Antioch.

Antioch students themselves sampled by *College and University Environment Scales* developed by C. Robert Pace of the University of California at Los Angeles, regarded the campus climate as highly intellectual, concerned with scholarly discipline, esthetic appreciation and expression, personal involvement with the world's problems.[2]

Why? and How? How can the Antioch system result in scholarly achievement above the majority of colleges devoting full time and energy to the most rigorous study? Antioch staff would answer that it is because that system is part of a total experimental approach to education.

The experimental approach has been in Antioch's history from its beginning in 1853. Horace Mann, experimenter, innovator in primary education, already famous for the Massachusetts system which would influence all future American education, gave up an eastern political career to come west as the first president of Antioch College. The program he attempted was not only experimental but also radical for the age and the region.

Horace Mann's Antioch entered areas of conflict, some of which are not yet resolved. The college would accept all qualified students, regardless of color, creed, or sex. Women would be educated on the same terms, enjoy the same rewards, as men;

ROBERT H. KNAPP and H. B. GOODRICH, *Origins of American Scientists*, University of Chicago Press, 1952.

ROBERT H. KNAPP and JOSEPH J. GREENBAUM, *The Younger American Scholar: His Collegiate Origins*, University of Chicago Press, 1953.

National Academy of Sciences, National Research Council, *Baccalaureate Origins of Doctorates in the Arts, Humanities, and Social Sciences Awarded in the United States, 1936-1950*, Washington, D. C., National Research Council, 1956.

National Academy of Sciences, National Research Council, *Baccalaureate Origins of Science Doctorates Awards in the United States, 1936-1950*, Washington, D. C., National Research Council, 1955.

GEORGE G. STERN, "Characteristics of the Intellectual Climate in College Environments," *Harvard Educational Review*, Vol. 33, No. 1 (Winter, 1963).

[2]For more detailed discussion of Pace's study, not yet published, see Antioch Catalog, 1964-1965, pp. 8-13.

so would Negroes be equal with whites. Truth would be pursued without restriction by creed or dogma.

The inevitable result of any such institution is conflict, and conflict there has been throughout Antioch's history.

But it was chiefly over finances and over conflicts in creed between two widely divergent philosophies, the Christian denomination which founded Antioch in 1852 and the Unitarians who came to its support, that the college almost foundered. The struggle to keep the college alive and unrestricted in intellectual and social freedom was too much for Horace Mann's precarious health. He died only six years after he became president, but Antioch survived largely because he had managed to solve its most pressing problems by buying the college back when it was sold at auction.

After Mann's death, Antioch's fires of experimentalism burned low. The college closed during the War Between the States. It reopened to continuing financial problems and was barely alive when Arthur Morgan in 1920 consented to become a trustee if he could be given a free hand in reorganization.

The new Antioch opened in 1921 with Arthur Morgan as president. The work-study plan or co-operative program was then and still is, forty-three years later, the single most striking feature of Antioch's experimental approach to education. And unlike most other "co-operative" colleges, Antioch's emphasis on work-study is primarily liberal education, not vocationalism or self-help.

Several of Antioch's experimental aspects will be described: first, the extramural program—that is, those parts of the total program which extend beyond the local campus as a geographical unit, to involve interaction of experience and study; second, academic or curricular experiments in classroom and laboratory—these also may extend far beyond the Yellow Springs campus with professors and crediting processes all over the world; third, what Antioch confusingly labels "community living"—those aspects concerned chiefly with inter-personal, social, and governmental matters on the campus in an attempt to engage the whole of life in the educational process.

I also want to mention here a fourth area, because it should be noted as part of the experimental climate: this is Antioch's promotion of, and involvement with, many ventures in co-operation with other organizations. In the most recent instance, Antioch is one of twelve members of the Great Lakes Colleges Association, concerned with developing resources in several areas not possible for one college alone; for example, expansion of curriculum, faculty, library, and programs abroad in non-western studies. Other developments in which Antioch either took the initiative, or co-operated, concern natural resources (an Outdoor Education Center, agricultural experiments, conservation); elementary and secondary education (school camping, the Antioch School, the National Science Foundation Teachers Program); industrial and professional research organizations (the former Antioch Industrial Research Institute, the Charles F. Kettering Foundation, the Fels Research Institute, Anthropology Research Project, Engineering Psychology Research Project); and cultural undertakings such as the Antioch Area Theater and the *Antioch Review*.

Although all these associated developments are very much related to Antioch's experimentalism, they would require separate volumes for adequate treatment and therefore will not be described further here.

No one innovation, not even the work-study plan itself, states the essence of Antioch's experimentalism. Rather, each item or program element is an externalization of a core of agreement which unites highly diverse and divergent fields, philosophies, and people, who, much as they may disagree on method, much as they may struggle over what or how much emphasis should be placed on program segments, still come together in their basic experimental approach.

This basis or core of agreement is not easy to state. It is not easily understood, even by newcomers to the Antioch faculty. It is far from universal or accepted in higher education. My own expression of it follows:

That education must be concerned with every aspect of life, especially human life;

That the unique quality and the right to free inquiry of every individual must be paramount, even when immediate institutional prestige is at stake;

That the aims, the processes, even, paradoxically, the most

cherished assumptions, are always open to question, examination, and reassessment, so long as these latter processes are themselves open and emotionally and intellectually honest; and that these rights apply to students as well as faculty and administrators;

That it is always possible to find a better way to achieve the Antioch aim—quality of education—and that it is the institutional obligation to try rather than to leave well enough alone.

This expresses what I think to be Antioch's genuinely experimental spirit. Whether one likes it, or approves of all of its manifestations, is immaterial. That the Antioch staff often has not sufficient foresight and wisdom to control its experiment, that some of its expressions have threatened its own survival, would, I think, be one of the few things agreed upon.

Thus far, both the institution and experimental approach survive. Those who have disagreed too violently or found the experimental way too upsetting to their manner of life have departed to more congenial ivy-clad halls.

Now for a more detailed look at the segments of the experiment. I have indicated the three areas into which we commonly and conveniently divide them—extramural, academic, campus living—and have noted, but will not discuss further, a fourth aspect.

By the very nature of the Antioch experiment, these areas cannot really be separated and should not be separated as much as they often are. The tendency to separation has always been a focal problem. But the three areas remain convenient subdivisions for verbal examination and are so used in the discussion to follow.

The Extramural Program

Arthur Morgan, like Horace Mann, already had a successful career when he came to Antioch. An engineer who was not himself a college graduate, he had noted what he thought were grave faults in higher education. He planned a new kind of college, to bring practicality and some comprehension of the sciences to humanities students, and to add humanities to technical programs. These additions would not be mere abstractions; direct practical experience would come to classroom and laboratory.

Alternating work and study, a plan used for engineering training at the University of Cincinnati, could be adapted to liberal arts and required of all students. They would try out occupations, acquire practical skills; they would experience economic, social, and technological forces by working with them. Employers would be teachers. Classroom instructors would use job experience (even, perhaps, their own) in their teaching. Students would continually bring their observations to class for questioning and examination. They would take back to jobs increasing knowledge, skills, awareness. They would grow in powers of observation and creativity at the same time they learned practicality, foresight, financial management. "Education in good proportion," "a budget for life," "educating the whole man," were terms often used to express Antioch aims.

These aims have remained central to the work-study philosophy and structure. But many changes have occurred in operation and applications.

Arthur Morgan envisioned small industries, selected for applicability to educational purposes, including the arts as well as business and research. Located near the college, they would employ students alternating between job and study, progressing from routine to responsible to management assignments. Such industries under practical, vigorous young idealists could transform communities, could solve financial problems for students and for the college. But financial and vocational aspects would never be paramount, only a proportioned part of a broad, liberal education, the apex of which was a life philosophy.

Antioch never really operated on the small industry plan, though there exists today, in Yellow Springs and elsewhere, a surprising number of organizations which originated in those early years.[3]

[3]Illustrative of these small industries are Antioch Bookplate Company, Antioch Press, Antioch Shoes, and the Morris Bean Company (an offspring of the Antioch Art Bronze Foundry). Later, in addition to the major Fels, Kettering, and other research operations already listed, the college was directly or indirectly responsible for Vernay Laboratories, the Yellow Springs Instrument Company, the Yellow Springs Clinic, and Metcalf Studios. The list could be continued at length.

From the beginning the college attracted students and staff of an experimental turn, but the plan developed almost immediately into something very different from the original design. Arthur Morgan could not himself administer and teach the whole program—and indeed it would have been contrary to his principles to control everything although he was often accused of doing so. Geographic spread of jobs became attractive, both because students and staff were drawn from the whole nation and because most of them preferred work in metropolitan centers if only as a change from the small village of Yellow Springs.

"Co-op jobs" were widely scattered as early as 1924-25 when students worked in 13 states. By 1934-35 they extended into 31 states. By various ingenious devices, the "co-op program" survived the depression. Enrollment increased steadily except for irregularities in war years. Antioch intended to remain small but the enrollment limitations went up to 750, then to 1200.

In 1963-64 slightly over 1700 students alternate between work and study every three or six months. At least half are always away from campus and the proportion away is larger now because of Antioch Education Abroad. In 1963-64 students came from all 50 states and 15 foreign countries. They worked for 580 organizations in 35 states and 25 foreign countries. Jobs are widely varied, from elementary through advanced, from arts and humanities to technical mathematics and physics, from secluded laboratories or forests to teeming crowds.

Thirteen extramural staff members, selected both for specialized knowledge of one or more fields and versatility as placement administrators and vocational counselors, handle the extramural program and continually explore each student's abilities and interests, personal needs and desires, and vocational hopes. The process is highly individualized, considering the magnitude of the task and the time limits. If to the student if often seems a struggle against an established order adapting very little to personal hopes and aspirations, to the staff the same process seems kaleidoscopic and shifting, hard to operate within practical limits.

The director of the extramural program recently described to the Antioch faculty "the squirrel-cage aspect of the administration of a program that arranges for 2000 short-term job placements per year for young people 17-22 years of age, requiring, as appropriate, simultaneous negotiation with assorted parents, deans, faculty advisers, alumni, police, psychiatrists, prospective employers, girl friends, boy friends."[4]

The student who survives to Antioch graduation—after five years alternating from campus to job and back again, making all the decisions necessary to each move—has probably had as rigorous a preparation for swift technological change in our shifting rural-to-urban society as any educational system could afford. He has had a very close look at his society unless he has deliberately shut his eyes. One of the basic work-study aims is certainly fulfilled.

This program is, however, a far cry from another original concept: the small-industry, small-community program by which individuals of high purpose were to transform their immediate environs and eventually their whole society. Whether the present system, with its emphasis primarily on adaptation to the cities with their corporations, unions, and mass media, will have influence in such direction—or whether any one college program could have—remains to be seen.

As for financial benefits, certainly work-study rarely enables a student to be self-supporting. For the institution, the present operations with their emphasis on high quality and on individualization are costly. No one has yet devised an inexpensive production method for 1700 individualized undergraduate programs with adequate quality controls. However, the program is less expensive than it might otherwise be because a student can earn at least his maintenance on his job and sometimes a good deal more and because the institution uses one plant and one staff for two student bodies.

The cooperative program has not been spared the challenge and questioning that I have described as basic to Antioch's experimental attitude. Unfortunately there has not yet been a complete qualitative and long-range study of Antioch graduates of the work-study program, though this has been a hope of

[4]Faculty Meeting Panel Discussion: "Co-op Program: What It Is and What It Might Become" by Mary Hunt, January 28, 1964.

many Antioch staff members.[5] But every study that has been done, plus evidence of increasing success of graduates who go on to advanced studies and into professions, has reinforced rather than weakened the place of work-study in the Antioch structure.[6] The institution has continued to be strongly committed to the system as an important liberal educational method.

International Expansions: Antioch Education Abroad

Antioch Education Abroad extends to other countries the basic principle that learning is most effective if it is both direct and personal and at the same time theoretical and analytical.

The idea of study abroad was neither new nor particularly experimental when the program was planned in 1956. The attempt to interweave various kinds of experiences abroad into a self-supporting part of an individualized degree program for students in all fields *was* experimental, however. It had to be varied, broadly based yet disciplined, with rigorously enforced standards; of modest cost with financial aids so that no student would be eliminated for financial reasons alone. It had to allow freedom of movement, yet be under sufficient administrative control to insure adequate advising and supervision as well as maintenance of institutional standards.

To many and especially to some most experienced in international education these features seemed mutually contradictory, even impossible. In operation, however, the program proved successful. It is still experimental but like the work-study plan itself it has found a large measure of support and acceptance and considerable enthusiasm at Antioch and abroad.

It became evident very early that neither financially nor administratively could a program for any number of participants

[5]See, for example, Algo D. Henderson and Dorothy Hall, *Antioch College: Its Design for Liberal Education*, Harper and Brothers, 1946. pp. 158-159.

[6]*The Antioch Graduate—A Study of His Career Planning and Later Work Adjustment* by Samuel Baskin, September, 1954, a comparative study of a group of Antioch and Oberlin graduates, was one of the first studies to present experimental evidence of the values of work experience as a significant contribution to the career planning process. There have since been other studies of the work-study program, but the long-range study remains to be done.

operate on an entirely individualized basis. In 1959-60, after analyzing and reviewing the experience of the previous two years, a sub-committee of the Educational Policy Committee approved administrative recommendations for a somewhat more limited and unified structure, but also reaffirmed basic aims and methods and endorsed the continuance of the program.

Antioch Education Abroad is still far from restrictive in comparison with the more usual Junior Year Abroad. During 1963-64 some 200 students participated in programs ranging from a three-month language and culture study in Guanajuato, Mexico—which, although it is taught and administered by Mexican professors, is run by Antioch so that a quarter can be directly substituted for a campus quarter—to nine-month university study plus three to six months of work and travel. Programs included nine European countries and nine countries of Africa, Asia, Latin America, and the Middle East. AEA has enrolled—and still does—students from all major fields.

Academically the program is considered primarily for general education. For some students it may also be valuable and decisive to a major field but this is not a primary Antioch aim. Language facility is required for university study in non-English speaking areas. The experience of living and studying in another language environment is regarded as one of the most valuable aspects of the program but the majority of participants are not foreign language majors. The pressures of preparation for the programs abroad have had great effect on the nature and staff of the foreign language department on campus.

Because of the nature and emphasis of this program, AEA has attracted a different range of students from those in most college programs abroad. For example, almost half are men and many, both men and women, are majors in the biological and physical sciences. Antioch's experience, therefore, will probably differ substantially from the results described in most of the studies to date of undergraduates abroad. There also is little doubt that AEA (with other factors both internal and external) has greatly influenced the "home" or on-campus curriculum in the degree of international and intercultural emphasis.

Thus far these judgments remain largely subjective, based on personal impressions and limited administrative and committee studies.[7] A survey of AEA alumni opinion is being conducted among the 400 who have graduated or withdrawn and the study will be continued with another 400 to 500 students still enrolled. Several more detailed and intensive studies of various parts of the program are also under way or contemplated.

Program for Young Adults from Abroad

Another international experiment is in a sense an outgrowth of Antioch Education Abroad because it began as a reciprocal program for young Germans in appreciation of employment assistance to Antiochians by the Carl Duisberg Gesellschaft.

The Special Educational Services Office administers this program with no relationship either to AEA or to the extramural department except that they are all responsible to the Dean of the Faculty and exchange information and services. The enrollment is now largely from German-speaking Europe but the emphasis is upon gradually widening international representation.

This program, as conducted by Antioch, has unique aspects. It utilizes in still another way the commitment to and experience with work as an integral part of education. This program tends to be vocationally oriented, however, since most participants have completed university or technical programs in their homelands and have some career experience. Some are sponsored by their own companies for the 15-21 month program which begins with three months on campus. Concentration is on language and introduction to the American social and cultural scene. Then follows 12 to 18 months employment by a United States organization. Placements are handled by the Antioch program director who makes occasional field visits. Students return to Antioch for two or three seminars during and at the end of the year to compare and analyze experiences.

The present operation will be expanded in 1965 by still another but differently scheduled program for teachers from abroad. The preparatory period will be longer, beginning in

[7]Information about the AEA programs may be found in *Antioch College Reports*, No. 3, "Undergraduate Experience Abroad (1957-61)," and a *Manual* published primarily for students in 1962.

January with three months on campus, followed by three spring months in Outdoor Education Centers and a summer of camp counseling and vacation. During their first six months participants will be interviewed and placed in United States schools to teach the following academic year. The degree of interest and acceptance by both home and state systems of education abroad has surpassed expectations and the program will begin in January, 1965.[8]

The Academic Curriculum

Arthur Morgan's plan for general education, and .the large proportion of time devoted to it out of the total curriculum, was as experimental—or at least as hotly argued—as was the work-study plan. Yet it, too, although revised many times, remains an integral part of the Antioch program.

Morris Keeton, now Dean of the Faculty, reviewed the situation in 1960:

> The notion that Antioch can educate the whole man has been more sharply debated during this study than at any time during the past fifteen years. Still the decision is, as before, to try, and, in trying, to devote some 50 per cent of our formal degree requirements to the non-specialist, non-vocational aspects of the student's education. Reflection upon, engagement in, and preparation for the life of citizenship, family membership, and personal fulfillment are entailed in what is here called general education. The study of great books and traditions, the survey of current human knowledge, and the broadening and deepening of students' interest and appreciations are all regarded as legitimate components to be duly emphasized in this task, but no one of them by itself is taken as the whole endeavor.[9]

The present system as revised in 1957 after the faculty review noted by Keeton may be summarized as follows. By a graduated

[8]For further descriptions of these two programs, see "A Different Kind of Discipline" by Freda and Irwin Abrams, *Overseas*, May, 1963; and two brochures published by Antioch College, *An International Work-Study Program for Teachers* and *An International Work-Study Program for Young Adults from Abroad.*

[9]*Antioch Restudied*, A Report on the Carnegie Study of the Antioch Educational Program, 1955 to 1960, published by Antioch College, August, 1960, p.3.

examination system at entrance and each year thereafter, students discover weaknesses to be remedied, or they waive requirements, or they may earn credit. Level I requirements in all three areas—humanities, social sciences, and physical sciences —must be completed before students pass on to Level II. Level III studies come only in the senior year and serve as a final integrating device, chiefly through seminars for which all fields take responsibility. Some seminar titles may indicate what is being attempted:

a. "Value Judgments by Mechanical Model"
b. "Social Psychology of Political Belief"
c. "Moving Mobile America"
d. "Myth, Metaphysics, and Culture"
e. "Arms Control and Disarmament"
f. "Anxiety and the Community of Man"
g. "The Science of Uncertainty"
h. "The Age of Pericles"
i. "The Community of Intellect"

The present system, adopted some years ago in lieu of the previous final comprehensive examinations in the senior year, is an attempt both to spread the load for student and faculty member and to continue to achieve some integration among disciplines and with the extramural program.

As in all educational institutions, the student eventually tackles a more intensive specialization in a field of concentration. When he enters his major field he must present a complete plan for satisfying all degree requirements; this in turn must be approved by the chairman of the field, by his extramural adviser and, if work or study abroad is part of his total degree plan, by the director of Antioch Education Abroad. The whole is checked by the registrar who points out any errors or inadequacies in the plan and, if there are deficiencies in his record, directs the student to remedial methods.

There has also been an effort through the years to recognize a wide variety of means for achieving either an introduction to or more intensive work within an area. These needs may be met by courses on the home campus, by Education Abroad (usually only after completion of all Level I requirements) or by independent study.

Independent study has been open to Antioch students since the reorganized program of 1921. Any student could declare his intention and get permission to study a course, or pass a requirement, quite outside the usual channels of classroom instruction. In practice, however, very few students took advantage of this opportunity. In recent years, therefore, the institution has been turning to official use of the device, with individual and group experiments to try out methods and gauge results, so that all students will have some experience with independent study before graduation.

Now under consideration at Antioch is an experimental program for the freshman year which, if it is adopted by the faculty, will incorporate independent study techniques into the entire program from the first year on.

Much of what is most experimental in the Antioch curriculum was discussed—or implied—in the first section: the experimental attitude, impacts of off-campus experience on the classroom, on the faculty, on content and organization of studies, on methods of presentation. Associated research projects and industries likewise enriched faculty and curricular range and greatly expanded intellectual interests and the intellectual environment.

Even so, the curriculum has never been as drastically experimental as Arthur Morgan hoped and intended. Competent staff come only from traditional universities as a rule, with a tendency to repeat traditional teaching methods. The most traditional methods, however, are bound to be challenged by the very calendar of operation[10] at Antioch, with its continual dis-

[10]Nothing has been subjected to more experimentation than the Antioch calendar, a perennial challenge to ingenuity of students and staff alike: "There *must* be a better way." Some of the liveliest battles have been fought over the calendar. The original five-week alternation was succeeded by various modifications of the five- then ten-week pattern; then three different versions of a quarter plan. At present the sequence extends over two years so that all students have a full six months on campus or on jobs in alternate years and faculty teach three quarters of a year. Any reader attracted to the exercise is invited to try constructing a system allowing for American family vacation patterns, and also for covering jobs at all times, dividing the student body into two equal portions—equal, that is, in terms of men and women, upperclass and underclass, major fields, and so on and on.

ruptions by two outsurging and insurging student bodies. To meet challenges that never comfortably cease, classroom instructors must be either ingenious or frustrated. They must also keep abreast of developments in their own fields if they are not to be further challenged by students whose jobs may have been concerned with new developments refuting former theories or information.

Many of the most successful Antioch teachers learn to *use* the disruptive sequences of the Antioch calendar in productive ways. For example, the Biology Department encourages students to turn a 10-credit campus course into 12 credits by adding a 2-credit project to be done in the job setting.

That we as individual staff members have not yet learned to utilize successfully all the program potentials, that we are continually both irritated and stimulated by our system—these are perhaps the chief incentives to experimentation. That the college as an institution is concerned with program evaluation and with research methods and ideas is indicated by its establishment of an Office of Program Development and Research. Reports published under its auspices indicate scope and direction: *Experiment in French Language Instruction; Experiment in Independent Study; Effecting Change in the College Student: Who Teaches What?; Using Groups in Independent Study; Undergraduate Research: The Sciences.*[11]

The Antioch Community

The third major part of the Antioch experiment is the community. Instead of a student government there is a community government. "Community" designates the total college, including all employees who work more than half-time and their husbands or wives. Non-faculty may apply for membership but are not obliged to participate; students and faculty are so obliged and their community fees are billed or subtracted from salary.

[11]*Antioch College Reports*, a series on new program developments and research studies published by the Antioch Office of Program Development and Research in Education, directed by Samuel Baskin, are "Experiment in French Language Instruction," No. 1; "Experiment in Independent Study (1956-1969)," No. 2; "Undergraduate Experience Abroad (1957-1961)," No. 3; "Effecting Change in the College Student: Who Teaches what?" No. 4; "Using Groups in Independent Study," No. 5; "Undergraduate Research: The Sciences," No. 6.

Membership rights and privileges are considerable, even from a monetary standpoint. Community government provides such services as a volunteer fire department and a campus bookstore. Fees cover admissions to almost all campus activities (concerts by local and outside artists, chorus, orchestra, and small ensembles); swimming and other widely varied games and sports, as well as folk-, square-, and social-dancing; AMPAC (Antioch Motion Picture Advisory Council which shows outstanding films); Antioch Area Theater and student workshop plays; a weekly newspaper; a literary magazine; programs of the Religion Committee.

Activities, however, represent only one segment of an attempt to incorporate all aspects of college living into a total educational pattern. An underlying objective is education for citizenship through responsible participation in government with opportunity to formulate and express opinion in all matters affecting the total community.

Community government itself is but one part of an unusual governmental structure. Under Ohio law the Board of Trustees is legally responsible for the college corporation; as is usual, it delegates much of its authority to the president. Antioch's president, however, shares authority with an Administrative Council made up of both faculty and students. The president and the dean of the faculty are ex-officio members. The faculty elects three representatives, and the community at large elects two more faculty members and three students. The Administrative Council has practical jurisdiction over the entire college operation; its power is considerable, more in actual operation than might be expected since legally (by amendment of the college charter in 1930) its function is only advisory to the president. It does have two unique prerogatives: (a) electing seven of the 28 trustees and (b) participating with the Board of Trustees in selecting the president.

The second governing body, the Community Council, is made up of six students and three faculty members, all elected by the community at large. The Community Council in turn appoints a community manager, a student who holds a paid full-time job and has three part-time assistants.

The community manager, his assistants, and the Community

Council with its committees administer an annual operating budget of over $70,000. They also work closely with the office of the dean of students on all aspects of Antioch life and activity: for example, the orientation of new students to the honor system as a method of common community agreement applying to all areas; the negotiation of standards for dormitory living and other aspects of community and individual behavior; and— a matter much discussed in recent months—decisions on codes affecting civil liberties for students as well as faculty.

Such a concept of government and of campus living requires both intelligent understanding and a high degree of individual responsibility with constant review and continual education and re-education of all community members alike.

As Antioch has grown larger with increasing turnover of staff and students, and as standards of behavior in the nation at large become more confused and confusing, so the operation of Antioch community agreements has become more difficult. Old methods are outmoded for they depended on small, compact campus groups living and working together in close personal association. New methods are needed, even for such a comparatively simple matter as determining and enforcing limitation of the community for its internal security. Visitors from surrounding areas can hardly be expected to understand and participate in the honor system as a matter of course. Should visitors therefore be eliminated? Or challenged? How? And by whom? These and other more perplexing problems have brought to a head the need to scrutinize and review the campus community structure in an effort to arrive at more workable methods and agreements without change in the basic philosophy.

The preparation and education of student leaders in the dormitories, especially of upperclass advisers to freshmen, have been revised and made more professional in psychological and anthropological terms. Various means to achieve representation of all resident halls in community government and in extramural policy considerations are recent experiments. So are various devices to bring faculty and students together in informal ways. The new freshman program now under consideration by the faculty and its committees will attempt to utilize more than ever before the potential of residence halls and student leadership.

Perhaps a fitting way to close this discussion and also to indicate the continuance of the experimental approach to problems in the community sphere as in other parts of the Antioch program is to quote from the May, 1964, *Antiochian*. This issue reviews for alumni some present problems as to institutional attitudes and responsibilities toward social and political action. The editor asks, in effect, "Should the college take the responsibility *in loco parentis?*" And President James P. Dixon replies:

At Antioch our concept of liberal education admits the possibility that the formal educational process can improve not only man's capacity to think but also his capacity to act. We have felt that in large measure the benefits of knowledge and disciplined habits of thinking were gained as a result of action. It is this belief that has supported the evolution of community government here and the direct engagement of students and faculty in making institutional decisions.

At the same time we have believed that the good life is best served by self-conscious attention to the exercise of individual freedoms. Because we do not believe that the way to learn the uses of freedom is to maintain authoritarian dependency upon parental figures, neither the faculty nor the deans of the college view students as dependent children, but rather as young adults.

In short we do not attempt to subsume a parental role. At the same time we do believe that the wisdom, experience, and ability of faculty should be made available to students as a resource in their learning of civic behavior just as much as it is a resource in their learning of intellectual behavior. It is for this reason, rather than any necessity or desire to play the parental role or to protect the institution from public criticism, that we have established within the Civil Liberties Code, which governs the whole Antioch community, procedures to govern the conduct of social and political action.[12]

[12]*The Antiochian*, May, 1964, "In Loco Parentis: The Evolution of an Imprecise Concept," p. 2.

Chapter 3

THE STEPHENS COLLEGE PROGRAM

By Ralph C. Leyden*

The Past

Stephens College belongs to today's group of "experimenting colleges"; it also belongs to the early group of experimental colleges. Although it began as a school for girls in 1833 and became Stephens College in 1870, its modern era began in the early 1900's under the leadership of James Madison Wood, President of Stephens College from 1912 to 1947, and that of W. W. Charters, Director of Research. Dedicated to the education of women, the College committed itself: (1) to a program fostering the growth and development of each student in terms of her own interests and the needs of society; (2) to providing a basic general education; (3) to stressing the central importance of religion; and (4) to fostering experimentation in teaching and programed development.

Roy Ivan Johnson in his book *Explorations in General Education* states the early convictions of the faculty and their leaders at Stephens in this way:

They believed that the business of general education is to fit the student for a successful and satisfactory life, as an individual and as a member of society. This belief dictates that education accept as its primary objective the development of individual attitudes and abilities necessary to competent and complete living. . . . They believed that the criterion for planning and implementing all learning experience must be the needs of the student. They believed that the essential needs and interests of men and of women are different in im-

---

*Mr. Leyden is Director of Educational Development, Stephens College, Columbia, Missouri.

portant ways and that therefore education for women must differ substantially from the training of men. They believed that in any need-centered program each individual student is the only valid frame of reference; and they reasoned that in such a program ways must be found to individualize instruction in order to satisfy the varying needs of individuals.

Consonant with these beliefs, the College contributed to two main streams in American education during the first half of the twentieth century—(1) the general education movement with its emphasis upon individual needs and differences as well as upon the needs of society and (2) the development of junior colleges. The College became known as an institution where new courses were being developed in the humanities, in the social studies, in communication, in marriage and the family, and in psychology in such a way as to relate the contributions of a given area to the interests and needs of students. It also became known as an institution where experimentation in more effective methods of instruction constantly accompanied the developments in program.

These emphases and beliefs have remained as permeating influences in the evolution of the Stephens pattern of education. They have guided the innovations which placed Stephens among the "experimental" colleges and which justify its being termed an "experimenting college" today.

The Present

Stephens College offers three degrees: the Associate in Arts, the Bachelor of Arts, and the Bachelor of Fine Arts. The major emphasis of the College in terms of numbers of students is on the program leading to the two-year Associate in Arts degree. It is intended that this program will continue to be a primary concern of the College. The Bachelor of Fine Arts degree is given in four fields: dance, music, fashion, and drama. It is expected that the enrollment in this degree program and in the Bachelor of Arts degree program will continue to be limited to a select group of students for whom these programs have particular advantages in terms of their aptitudes, interests, and goals.

To carry out its program of education the College offers

courses specifically designed to contribute to the general education of the student through a wide range of liberal studies and
specialized courses in certain pre-vocational and vocational
areas, including those of the Bachelor of Fine Arts curricula.
The student's Associate in Arts program is almost entirely elective, but each student plans her program in consultation with
her faculty adviser who maintains a counseling relationship
with her throughout her years at the College. The heart of the
general education program is the set of basic courses. These
consist of English 1-2, General Humanities, Contemporary Social Issues, The Contemporary American Woman, Basic Beliefs in Human Experience (Philosophy 1-2), and Fundamentals
of Natural Science. With the help of her adviser the student
chooses from among these basic courses and adds to them other
courses which will enable her to achieve some depth of understanding in her special interest, whether this be in the field of
liberal studies or pre-professional training or, as is most usual,
both.

In carrying out its concern for the individual growth and development of each student, the College gives more than usual
attention to the out-of-class opportunities for learning. Each
hall has its own resident counselor, trained in personnel work,
who works directly with students in the group-living aspects of
their education. The activities of the residence halls are integrated under the Civic Association, the student government
organization, which is given a grant of power by the President
for carrying out the functions of self-government. The extraclass activities of students which are beyond those in the residence hall are also matters of concern and the College provides
faculty sponsorship and guidance for them.

Under a Dean of Religion the College carries out its commitment to the importance of religion by providing a varied
program of religious experiences—vespers, Sunday morning
services, evening prayer, hall meditation periods, and special
convocations with religious emphasis. In addition, a student
organization conducts a program known as the Burrall Program
which includes a wide variety of opportunities for students to
engage in social service projects within the community and
surrounding territory. The Burrall Program also includes stu-

dent arranged seminars, conferences, and other special events which enable students to probe deeply into their own personal beliefs and commitments.

In carrying out its commitment to a continuous program of educational experimentation and research, the College encourages the undertaking of special projects which have specific implications for teaching and learning and also programs of study in which faculty members have particular scholarly interests. Each summer the College awards grants in both of these activities. Frequently as many as one-third of the faculty will be engaged in summer study extending from a week or two to much of the summer. Some projects are conducted as workshops with several staff members participating; others constitute individual assignments, the results of which will be shared with colleagues. The individual awards given faculty often involve foreign travel or an opportunity to study off-campus or to write. In these ways the College seeks to foster a climate conducive to development of constantly more effective and efficient teaching.

Experimentation and Development

Today the program of experimentation and development at Stephens College might be described as falling under three categories: (1) program development, (2) innovation and improvement in teaching, and (3) design and construction of new facilities for learning. Obviously, all three categories are closely related and the activities under one occasion the need for or influence the activity under another category.

Program Development

In carrying out its commitment to providing a general liberal education, especially during the first two college years and culminating in an Associate in Arts degree, the College has given constant attention to the development of a series of basic courses. Some of these have served in the past as prototypes for other institutions. During the past four years the College has given particular attention to the analysis, revision, and development of the following set of basic courses.

The *General Humanities* course has a three-fold objective: (1) to increase the number of arts the student enjoys and understands including architecture, literature, music, painting, sculpture, and the combined arts; (2) to develop the realization that there are certain basic principles common to all art; (3) to introduce the student to means of formulating judgments of what comprises a valid artistic expression so that she may continue to apply what she has learned. The text for the course, written by Louise Dudley—founder of the course—and Austin Faricy, has been frequently revised and is widely used in other colleges.

Foundations of Natural Science, the basic course in that area, has been and is undergoing an intensive reorganization and development. Through an interdisciplinary approach in the sciences, the course seeks to provide insights into the scientific process in contrast to the usual acquaintance with only the scientific product. In this course the epistemological structure of science is meshed with the presentation of the "most" significant concepts in the sciences. The course is developed in a "logical" structure starting with the nature of matter and energy, which becomes the necessary foundation upon which to build an understanding of cellular dynamics—cellular, organismic, and species continuity—and biotic and environmental interrelationships. It deals with both process and product. Laboratory work allows the student to gather first-hand experiences in the attack on problems and the management of physical apparatus, both simple and complex, in the emancipation of data.

Basic Beliefs in Human Experience, the beginning course in philosophy, is particularly indigenous to Stephens. Starting from the premise that philosophical and religious concerns are of great importance in human existence, the objective of the course is to make the student aware of our philosophic roots and aware of the perennial and basic questions man asks. It has as its goal the development of a philosophic attitude and of a personal philosophy in the life of the student.

A course titled *The Contemporary American Woman* is the newest among the basic courses at the College. Its objective is to acquaint the young woman with some of the major and important facts about woman's historic role in our own culture and, comparatively, in other cultures. With such a background the course helps the student identify and analyze the role and problems of the contemporary American woman. Together with the course, *Marriage and Family*, it attempts to give students an understanding of what today's culture may demand of them and of what opportunities exist for self-realization.

The *Contemporary Social Issues* course sets as its objectives: (1) to introduce the student to the basic contemporary social issues which every American must face; (2) to teach the individual how to study controversial social questions calmly and intelligently with an emphasis upon rational analysis rather than upon emotion and prejudice; and (3) to develop in the individual such a profound interest in the solution of these issues that she will always take an active—and hopefully intelligent—part in civic life. Through extensive required reading and much class discussion the following topics are treated: The Nature of Social Change, Democracy and the "Isms," The Politics of American Democracy, Personal and Social Disorganization, Race and Cultural Minorities, The American Economic System, American Foreign Policy, and Living in the Mass Society.

English 1 and 2—formerly *Communication*—through instruction in both written and oral communication, though primarily the former, concentrates on the study of the functions of mind: inquiry, judgment, and a representation of passion. The course syllabus describes these functions in the following manner:

(1) The process of inquiry involves the student in a study of informal logic and the principles of investigation. He is expected to demonstrate his ability in inquiry by preparing an investigative paper drawing his subject from any of the academic disciplines. (2) The process of judgment takes the student beyond the determination of what is and into a consideration of worth or value. He studies the techniques of persuasion as the means of organizing logical inquiry to substantiate careful judgment. (3) A study of the representation of passion through literary expression brings the student to a consideration of poetry, drama, and fiction. He studies literature as a means of communication: a use of language which allows a common, symbolic participation into the emotional life of other men.

Ideas and Living Today

A course titled *Ideas and Living Today* is illustrative of program innovation at Stephens. Inasmuch as the curriculum at Stephens is primarily elective, the faculty felt a need to develop a required course which would give students a common forum for the discussion of important ideas. Consequently, the course titled Ideas and Living Today was developed with the objective of providing an introduction to a liberal education. Drawing its subject matter from contemporary issues in the arts, in science, in the social sciences, it attempts to give students an introduction to the meaning of a liberal education. Closed circuit television is the medium chosen for teaching the course. This was necessitated by a desire to have all students hear the same presentation simultaneously. Following twenty-minute presentations by television, small groups of students discuss the topic under the leadership of a member of the faculty. These faculty members are drawn from all departments in the College.

The House Plan

The House Plan of organization is another example of program experimentation and development. Initially begun under a grant from the Ford Foundation, this plan of organization has now become a regular part of the Stephens program. Essentially it is a plan whereby approximately 100 students are assigned to a given dormitory. Previously they have elected to take a common core of subjects: General Humanities, Basic Beliefs in Human Experience, Contemporary Social Issues, and English. In addition they take the required course, Ideas and Living Today. Five faculty members are assigned to the residence hall. They teach the courses mentioned to the students in the hall and serve as their advisers. One of the group is the resident hall counselor. Through this plan the College attempts to relate constructively the activities of both living and learning. Inasmuch as the major program of the students is conducted by a small group of faculty, it is possible to give the group considerable autonomy in the planning of schedules, teaching programs, experimentation, and other activities. The group has employed a wide range of methods of teaching: independent study, concentration periods when no classes are held, supervised field study in New York City, programed learning, large group instruction, and conference teaching. Several of these innovations are being adapted in other parts of the campus.

Bachelor of Fine Arts

Recently inaugurated at Stephens College is the Bachelor of Fine Arts program. This is a program in which students work continuously through three academic years and two summers. The course of study combines specialization with . extensive study in the liberal arts. The fields in which a degree may be taken include dance, theater, music, and fashion design.

Bachelor of Arts

The most recent inclusion in the Stephens program is the Bachelor of Arts degree. In the Bachelor of Arts program the student chooses a field of concentration and in consultation with the head of the appropriate division develops a detailed schedule of activities. These include both common and specialization seminars as well as a combination of courses, drawn from the various departments of the College, which have demonstrable meaningfulness in terms of the specific personal and educational goals of the candidate. The traditional major and minor sequences are not employed.

Continuing Education

In keeping with its dedication to the education of women, the College has studied and continues to study what role it might reasonably play in contributing to the continuing education of women generally and of its graduates in particular. The faculty of the humanities department developed an adult education series which was widely used. Currently the College is conducting week-long seminars for women and is cooperating with universities in large metropolitan centers to acquaint Stephens alumnae with the educational opportunities existing and available to them.

The above examples serve as illustrations of various approaches to program development at Stephens College. This development is not limited, however, to the examples given. Experimentation and restudy are constantly encouraged.

Innovation and Development in Teaching

Many areas of instruction illustrate the constant emphasis upon teaching improvement at Stephens College.

Language. During the past three years instruction in beginning languages has undergone a radical revision. Basing the reorganization on modern structural linguistics, members of the staff have employed an intensive aural-oral approach. They have developed a varied and extensive accompaniment of visual aids. They have adapted automated devices, such as the Perceptoscope, to the showing of both still and motion pictures intermittently in order to convey better the meanings of vocabulary and of more complex concepts. They have employed both language-learning laboratories and telephonic listening stations around the campus.

Science. In science the staff has developed a programed laboratory manual to replace stereotyped traditional manuals. Lectures, accompanied by original photography mounted in slides, have been made available to both instructors and students through automation. These materials are used both in class instruction and in independent study. Presently they include series on evolution and on ecology. Currently also the science faculty is experimenting with both large group and team teaching techniques.

Programed Instruction. Programed materials have been developed for units in the teaching of logic and have been used both in the course Basic Beliefs in Human Experience and in freshman English. Other materials have been developed for review and for instruction in fundamentals of English.

Amplified Telephone Instruction. One of the most exciting and interesting experiments in teaching has been that employing the amplified telephone technique. Starting from initial experimentation in the teaching of government classes in 1958, the College has used lecturers and interviewees in courses in social studies, business, philosophy, literature, and mathematics. During the year 1963-64 an experiment involving the teaching of three different courses for a group of eleven cooperating colleges was conducted at Stephens. The three courses included a seminar on the Teaching of Science, a course titled Great Issues in Contemporary Society, and a third course American Life as Seen by Contemporary Writers. In each of these courses the program emanated from the Stephens campus but the master teachers of the courses spoke from their homes or offices from all over the United States and in some instances from abroad. Thus the faculty of the courses represented a truly international "who's who" kind of faculty. The experiment was underwritten by a special grant from the Fund for the Advancement of Education. It demonstrated that it is possible and feasible for a group of interested colleges to employ the services of otherwise unattainable individuals. Since all the colleges in this experiment have very modest resources, several of them being Negro colleges, the technique shows promise of increasing the faculty resources of such institutions.

Automated Instructional Materials. In the General Humanities course members of the teaching faculty make much use of many and varied visual and audio materials. One of the more interesting developments has been the preparation of lecture materials on tape recordings synchronized, where this is useful, with slides. Series have been developed on the principles of architecture, the geometry of style in painting, and the techniques of drawing. Audio-tapes have been developed for the teaching of the basic principles of music. Elements in the theory of music are being taught in an experimental section through the use of overhead projectors. In this experiment students work with an overhead projector when doing classroom exercises in original compositions. The technique permits the instructor to project, for all to see, the work of any given student for analysis and criticism.

Television. Television is increasingly used in instruction. A series of 13 lectures has been recorded on videotape to be used as a core of instructional materials in the freshman English course. Projected are similar lecture series in The Contemporary American Woman course, in humanities, and in psychology. Closed circuit television is also employed for the showing of assigned films in the child study course. Even in the extraclass program of the College, closed circuit television serves as the medium of instruction during the early orientation periods in each college year.

Patterns of Teaching. Several other variations in teaching are receiving current attention at Stephens. Several different patterns of the scheduling of classes are being tried out under the House Plan organization. Most of the divisions of the College are experimenting with the teaching of large classes for lecture presentations. These are supplemented by small group discussions and individual conference sessions. Another pattern being explored in several areas is team teaching. First tried in the required televised Ideas and Living Today course, the technique is being exploited particularly in the teaching of beginning psychology.

Having had a long interest in and use of audio-visual aids to teaching, the faculty of Stephens has been experimenting with the utilization of some of the newer media. These experiments and the availability of the newer educational media have greatly influenced the third category of experimentation and development—new facilities for learning.

Physical Facilities for Learning.

The third category that represents innovation and development at Stephens is the area of planning and building new facilities for instruction. The new learning center in the James Madison Wood Quadrangle represents one of the more unique new facilities on the college campuses of the nation. It was chosen as one of the twelve outstanding facilities to be included in the Airborne Institute conducted under the auspices of the School Planning Laboratory in the summer of 1964.

Planning of the learning center was greatly aided by substantial grants from the Educational Facilities Laboratories. First, a conference titled *New Frontiers in Learning* was held. Out of this conference of nationally-known educators and others interested in the future of education grew the principles used as guidelines for the planning of the facilities. The principle of *flexibility* was applied to the design of spaces and buildings in anticipation of the changes expected to occur in the pattern of educational needs. Several spaces are designed to serve multiple purposes—designed to be used in as many ways and for as many purposes as the College's educational demands require and architectural design makes feasible. Another basic principle of planning was that of providing for a *variety* of both resources and spaces. The learning center provides for the tremendous new range of resources—films, records, video-tapes, slides, and combinations of these in addition to the old and proven resources of books and people. The basic principles of *ready availability* of materials and *close proximity* of materials, spaces, and people were also observed in the planning. The five buildings of the Quadrangle are all connected at one level. The relationship between classrooms, offices, seminar rooms, library, and laboratories is enhanced by their being related parts of a unified plan.

The objectives which further governed the design and equipping of the learning center were:

1. To create an environment most favorable to learning.
2. To provide space and facilities designed for versatility and maximum utilization.
3. To make available the wealth of modern resources in educational materials and aids for study of the arts and sciences.
4. To encourage the student in her capacity for self-education.
5. To enable the teacher to utilize his time and ability more effectively.

Primary Features of the Learning Center

Of primary importance in the design and equipping of the learning center is the basic communication system which forms the electronic heart of the facility. A dual coaxial cable augmented by many pairs of audio wires permits the sending and receiving of audio and visual signals throughout the entire center. It is possible to originate or receive television in any classroom or laboratory and in any auditorium, gallery, or library area. The inclusion of electronic and mechanical aids in the Stephens learning center is based upon a "systems" approach to the use of technology in education. This design incorporates the large scale communication system just mentioned together with a variety of meaningfully related educational media devices. The entirety makes available and feasible a multi-media support of both discrete and interrelated fields of instruction. Each classroom, teaching auditorium, or lecture room constitutes a sub-system. In each of these spaces an electronic console permits the teacher to control from his desk the tuning in of television; the projection from slide, tape, or film strip projectors; the receiving or playing of phonograph recordings or taped recordings and control of sound—either stereophonic or monaural; and the lighting. By having his illustrative material preset or programed in advance, the instructor has at his command any desired variety of illustrative and supporting materials he may wish.

The entire learning center is so designed as to provide a range of sizes of space for differing instructional purposes. Faculty offices are of such a size as to permit small seminar groups of five to 10 students, classrooms will accommodate up to 40-45 students depending upon the formality of seating arrangement. Pairs of classrooms divided by operable walls may be used individually or thrown together to accommodate as many as 80-90 students. An arena classroom, also divisible by an operable wall, will accommodate 60 students in each half or 125-150 as a single room. This room also is so designed as to permit its use for theater-in-the-round. A lecture theater will accommodate 128 students. It is also capable of doubling as a small recital area or actor's theater. A 300-seat teaching auditorium provides for large group instruction and previously existing auditoriums accommodate 600 and 2,900 persons respectively.

The largest and physically the most dominating building of the learning center is the resources library. Its ground floor is integrated with the master communication system. Here an under-floor network of ducts makes possible the installation of any electronic device that may prove useful to teaching or learning. This floor is equipped with learning carrels similar in style and equipment to language laboratory booths. Here the student can study pre-assigned recorded material. She can check out individual television sets for programed material. Here also are listening rooms accommodating 3-4 students where they may play materials assigned for study in the humanities, drama, English, or other subjects. Here too are carrels so designed as to provide wall space for the display of pictures which are later checked out for student use in dormitory rooms. These display areas then convert into carrels.

The three remaining floors of the library contain open stacks, many secluded reading and study areas, individual carrels, browsing areas, conference rooms, and an informal reading area around an open fireplace on the top floor of the library. Carpeted throughout, the library is an experiment in providing pleasant surroundings which are highly conducive to concentrated study and intensive learning. The attempt has been to create a non-institutional appearing but institutionally functioning library facility. The design and arrangement of furnishings and the equipping with the full range of learning resources from automated devices to time-proven books makes it such a place.

The Stephens College learning center project is especially significant because of its departure from previous educational patterns. The Educational Facilities Laboratories has commented: "There have never been gathered together on an American campus all such means of instruction. This attempt to saturate one (area) with all the tools available and appropriate for instruction should help answer many questions . . . ."

The Future

In 1959-60 the faculty and administration of Stephens College engaged in a college-wide self-study. As a result of this study the College has projected a ten-year plan. Significant features of this ten-year plan include increase of the College enrollment to approximately 2,400 or 2,500 (in comparison to the present 1,850). This growth is expected to occur primarily in the upper division of the College whose programs lead to the Bachelor of Arts and the Bachelor of Fine Arts degrees. To accommodate this increase a new dormitory quadrangle is being erected; its design is influenced by the College's experience with the desirability of closely relating living and learning as in the House Plan organization. The College looks forward to an increasing strengthening of its faculty and a continuing encouragement of better teaching and constant program development. Finally, the College looks forward to a continued identification as an experimenting college. In a statement re-affirming the historical educational stance of Stephens College and projecting its commitments into the future, President Seymour A. Smith expressed his views on the need for the experimenting college:

> Our hope, as I see it, lies in the possibility of the emergence of a great number of institutions, large and small, infected with the experimenting spirit. Actually this is already coming about, for many of the larger institutions are being forced into experimenting with new patterns, new methods and new resources by virtue of the almost impossible situations they currently confront. . . . For the good of higher education we need a host of institutions working on one or several of the more promising avenues for improving learning, trying new patterns, doing the necessary research, and sharing their experiences with others.

Stephens College, in its looking to the future and through its ten-year plan committing itself to this task, hopes that in addition to serving its own student body it may make some contributions to education at large.

Chapter 4

NEW COLLEGE: D MINUS FIVE MONTHS

By JOHN W. GUSTAD*

A puzzling, frustrating, but probably vitalizing characteristic of American higher education is its diversity. The array includes giant universities—the multiversities described by President Clark Kerr of the University of California—both public and private in control; state colleges; liberal arts colleges; technical institutes; teachers colleges; junior and community colleges. While the members of each class have certain things in common, their differences are enormous. There is no need here to comment further; everyone is familiar with the range.

The remarks to follow will be concerned with *one* attempt to create *one* college within *one* of the classes: liberal arts colleges. The attempt to create a liberal arts college, however, has brought those concerned with New College face-to-face with the knotty problem of reaching a viable definition of liberal education. Actually, if one considers the operating policies and procedures of a college a de facto operational definition of its view of liberal education, there are as many definitions as there are liberal arts colleges. On the other hand, one can readily observe certain communalities which justify reducing the number of definitions substantially. In a sense, liberal arts colleges are like people: black or white, tall or thin, male or female, young or old—there is something human about them. When one tries to reach for this human essence, however, it proves to be exceedingly elusive. I would submit that this is so in large part because somehow the essence of liberal education is human, a mercuric, phantasmagoric, but very real entity.

Not to be diverted into an attempt to speculate in this

---

*Mr. Gustad is Provost and Dean of the College, New College, Sarasota, Florida.

philosophical thin air, it seems fair to try to describe one college's attempt to arrive at a working definition of liberal education and to implement this with a program. There is no need
here to essay any systematic coverage of the history of liberal
education. In deference to the fact that this is a conference
populated by scholars, however, it would be only seemly to
make passing reference to Athens in its golden age.

First, however, let me state a thesis: while liberal education
is multi-dimensioned, two of the most important dimensions—
or would it be better to call them sides of the same coin or, to
acknowledge (if it is so) orthogonality, the warp and woof?—
might be labeled as (1) the concern for content and (2) the
concern for individual development. Let me make it clear at
the outset that I do not consider these to be opposed in any
essential way although in practice one may gain such ascend-
ance that it is detrimental to the other.

By concern for content I mean the age-old belief that part
of the business of higher education is to preserve, to cull, to
criticize, and to add to man's store of knowledge. It is this concern which results in the assignment of such importance to
libraries, laboratories, and research on campuses. Surely, to be
educated means to know some things which the knower and
others believe worth knowing.

The concern for individual development is less often openly
acknowledged to be an explicit goal (except in such vacuous
notions as the "well-rounded man"), but it has been, I would
insist, an important, sometimes dominating thread in the fabric
of education. It was so, long before John Dewey came on the
scene. It is harder to describe succinctly or satisfactorily. It is
to be seen as a theme in the Platonic dialogues, particularly in
the *Republic*, where the education of the philosopher-kings is
not only concerned with what they know but with the kinds
of persons this knowledge *and its acquisition* makes of them.
It may be seen in the history of Oxford and Cambridge where,
often, what the graduate knew was of much less importance
than what he was.

Viewed in one way, this concern views education as a kind
of rite of passage, an initiation into the establishment with the
college serving as a useful but in some ways substantively irrele-

vant screening and polishing agent. At its best, this concern for individual development was well expressed by Sir Francis Bacon who said that we should not worry about educating lawyers, teachers, or physicians but rather thinking men who are *also* lawyers, teachers, and physicians. I will not belabor this distinction further; I hope and trust that the points are reasonably clear.

Colleges differ among themselves as to the emphasis they put on each of these concerns; they differ individually over time within each institution. These concerns were, in a sense, involved in Socrates' quarrel with the sophists, for he was interested mainly in getting young men to think deeply and imaginatively while the sophists were selling a set of socially desirable skills and items of information. Let me repeat: I am suggesting no basis for invidious comparison between these two concerns. I believe that properly conceived liberal education demands the presence of *both*. What I am suggesting is that these are best dealt with if recognized explicitly and taken into account.

One other problem needs brief examination as part of the preamble. The ubiquitous explosion of knowledge has brought colleges to a point where new solutions, more adaptive than the mere addition of courses of instruction, must be sought. Curricula are in desperate need of thorough revision. It also seems to be a propitious time to realize that no one can know everything and that the best that a college can hope to do for its graduates is to equip them with an adequate supply of vital ideas and functional skills which will permit them to continue their educations throughout their lives.

So much for prologue. Now for New College. In the earliest discussions among the founders of New College certain broad policies were laid down. One was the decision to operate on a year-round basis, permitting graduation in three calendar years. Another specified that the students would pay the actual cost of instruction. A third required that all students be in residence. A fourth policy—actually less of a policy than a belief— pointed to extensive use of the tutorial mode of instruction. Within these broad outlines, New College has developed to its present point.

Year-round operation is certainly a rapidly developing trend in higher education. The traditional academic year is a fossil relic of days when young men needed to be freed for haying and harvesting on the farms. Its persistence is due in part to the vast inertia of the institution but is, without design but with success, attuned to the fact that uninterrupted study makes for dull boys. Various forms of year-round calendars such as the trimester and the four quarter plan are beginning to encounter a considerable amount of resistance. Faculty members and students are increasingly finding ways to build in breathing periods.

On the other hand, it is hard to justify the traditional academic calendar in a day when millions of students need—or, at least, want—higher education and when funds for new buildings and new faculty are so inadequate and when faculty members with even nominal qualifications are at a premium. The opportunity and the challenge for New College were to discover a calendar which had the virtues of real efficiency and yet which took into account the facts of life regarding need for rest, rehabilitation, and rumination.

The calendar on which we propose to operate involves a forty-eight week year. Starting in late September, it will consist of three twelve-week terms with each term followed by a four-week independent study period. Students will normally be expected to commit themselves to forty-eight weeks, but they may, if it seems in their best interests on any of a number of bases, take off a term or a reading period. Faculty members will be permitted to take off any two of the three reading periods; in addition, provision will be made for scholarly leave on a more extended basis.

One major goal which such a calendar seems likely to attain is that of flexibility. We have, for instance, little or no interest in the junior year abroad or any of its variations. An opportunity to go abroad is probably a good thing but under different conditions. Under the present conditions of travel, it would be possible to send a student to Oxford to work with a specialist on a topic of interest to him and have the student do a significant piece of work within a month. This is particularly true if, as planned, he spends the previous term working up a problem to a fairly advanced point. However, if more time is required, he could take a twelve week term. Or, he could combine a term and a reading period for sixteen weeks. He could, if desired, add on the previous reading period for a total of twenty weeks. The system is modular and highly flexible. This was the goal.

A college can do no better than to prepare its graduates for a lifetime of disciplined and productive use of intelligence. Facts become obsolete, but the acquisition of certain principles and analytical processes can become the student's most valuable graduation gift. The New College program is intended fundamentally to permit and encourage students to attain a power and competence in intellectual analysis and a deeply rooted desire to go on learning which together will enable them to lead free and exciting lives.

Several basic assumptions have led to the creation of the New College curriculum:

1. Each student is responsible in the last analysis for his own education.

2. The best education results from the active confrontation of two first class minds. The emphasis here must be on "active" and "first class." A former president of Fisk University said that to put a second rate teacher into a small class results only in the passing on of mediocrity under conditions of intimacy.

3. The greater the degree of flexibility, the greater is the likelihood that students will reach the highest levels of which they are capable. It was the search for flexibility that led to the creation of the calendar already described. It led to a decision to teach only a very small number of courses. It serves as a guide in developing the entire program.

4. Student progress should be based on demonstrated competence and real mastery rather than on the accumulation of credits and grades. Too often, students are permitted to proceed with only C-minus competence or 75 per cent mastery. At New College, we expect to demand that the students proceed as quickly as they can but to demonstrate before they go on that they do in fact have control of a topic or area.

5. The best liberal education derives from such mastery of a small number of vital ideas, principles, and modes of analysis.

Higher education's stables are urgently in need of a Hercules to clean out the accumulated debris, what Whitehead called "inert ideas." Since no one can know everything, it is better to teach little but teach that supremely well.

6. Liberal education requires an appreciation for the unity of knowledge.

7. Students should have from the very outset opportunities to explore in depth areas which are of interest to them. Some will have a good idea when they enter of what they want to study; others will need a period of exploration. Basic to this assumption is opportunity.

The curricular structure of New College is as follows. In the first year students will be required to take three courses: one in the natural sciences (including mathematics approximately through the calculus), one in the social sciences, and one in the humanities (including foreign language). In addition, they may (although this will not be required) take an additional course in some discipline which interests them. At the end of the first year for most (later for some, perhaps earlier for a few), there will be a series of comprehensive examinations. Those familiar with the Chicago system will see some resemblances.

The second year will see approximately two-thirds time devoted to the specialty area, the rest to electives. Students will be expected to continue to read widely in areas outside of their specialties. Reading lists and preceptors will guide them. In addition, they will be expected to use the language they have mastered to read both in their specialties and also in the masterpieces of that language.

The last year will be devoted in part to the specialty, including a piece of independent research, and in part to an interdisciplinary seminar designed to encourage the bringing to bear of insights acquired all along the spectrum of the disciplines.

It is expected that students will take no more than two or at most three seminars at any one time. These will not be "content" seminars but will deal, rather, with modes of analysis. For instance, we do not expect to have a course in American history. Not that American history is not important. It is. It is too important to be treated as it usually is. The student who has learned to read history with insight and perception, however, can be left very largely alone to accumulate the essential body of facts.

From the very outset, tutorial experiences will be made available. The relationship we hope to foster between students and faculty is that of colleagues. To some extent, this will produce changes in the traditional tutorial pattern familiar from Oxford. Nevertheless, we believe that it is in the one-to-one relationship of the tutorial that the most exciting education is likely to take place.

Any college—even one still in embryonic form—is a complex affair, and there are many aspects of New College which invite comment. The quality of the faculty and the student body are absolutely crucial. Something can be said about both now, but it seems better to wait. The proof of the pudding is still in the eating.

One area, however, involves an enormous risk but one which we view as essential to take. That is the intent to dispense with credits and grades. Credits as measures of student or faculty work load are very largely meaningless. There is almost no variance. Grades have been an albatross around the necks of faculty members and students alike. Numerous studies have demonstrated the unreliability of grades. Those of you familiar with measurement theory will recall that the validity of a measure cannot exceed the square root of the reliability. This casts grave doubt on the validity of grades.

Even worse, however, grades serve to conceal more than they reveal. In all but large lecture courses, conscientious professors manage to learn a good bit about students. At the end, however, this must be compressed into a single letter grade or number. In the conditions we expect to have at New College, we feel that what the professor knows must not be ground up and reduced to a single index.

Another bad feature of the usual grading system is that it puts the students and faculty into a kind of competition and makes difficult the development of colleagueship. The credits and grades, rather than the learning they presumably reflect, become the ultimate goals of students.

In hopes of avoiding the pressures to conform to usual practice, New College proposes to dispense with a registrar and to have instead a college examiner. John W. French of the Educational Testing Service will assume this responsibility. His responsibilities will be two-fold: first, to select where appropriate and develop where necessary a whole range of evaluative devices—tests, rating scales, anecdotal records, and the like—to generate as complete a picture as possible of student progress; second, to initiate and maintain an imaginative and thoroughgoing program of research on a whole range of problems, providing those concerned with the information by means of which programs may be modified as seems indicated. If there is a key job at New College, it is his.

In broad outline, this is New College less than a half year before it opens. The problems of creating any new college are enormous. The problems of creating a genuinely distinguished college are almost unbelievable. If it were easy to do, it would have been done many times. One has only to look at the handful of great colleges to be assured that any effort is more than justified; it is required.

Chapter 5

PARSONS COLLEGE: EXPERIMENT AS THE ART OF THE POSSIBLE

By Lee Sutton*

In order to understand the Parsons College experiment it is first necessary to understand the kind of college it is and the kind of experiment which has been conducted.

In 1955 Parsons was a typical, midwestern, church related, privately supported "liberal arts" college. The bulk of its students were actually being trained professionally; enrollments in teacher education and business courses helped maintain the small liberal arts program. The elective tradition had encouraged course proliferation until at one time there were more than 700 courses listed in the catalog. The ratio of students to teachers was low; very small classes were the rule rather than the exception.

The student body was drawn almost entirely from the immediate area. Theoretically there was some screening of applicants; in actuality few high school graduates were denied admission. The attrition rate was high. Graduates were generally well trained but few in number.

In almost all of its aspects, even in its deficits, Parsons was typical of hundreds of such small, accredited, privately supported colleges.

It seems to me there are two general kinds of educational experiments. The first kind sets for itself ideal goals and tries to achieve them with ideal methods. The experimenters ask "What *ought* we do?" and "What are the best methods of doing this?" Parsons experiment was of another kind. Both methods and goals started with an objective situation. The questions

---

*Mr. Sutton is Librarian and Professor of Library Science, Parsons College, Fairfield, Iowa.

were "What *can* we do?" and *"How* can we do it?" In this latter
kind of experiment both ends and means are subject to continuous modification, since the ability to do something may
change and in a moving situation methods are quickly seen to
be workable or unworkable. To describe the Parsons College
experiments in ideal terms would be to misrepresent the values
of what has actually been achieved.

The new administration of President Millard G. Roberts
faced an educational situation that was dubious and a financial
situation that was close to impossible.

What were the actual goals of the college, contrary statements
notwithstanding? These goals were to take students of all levels
of ability and train, inform, and educate them. The emphasis
was on training for teaching or business. These students were
to be made useful, informed, and, possibly, thinking citizens.
These are limited goals, but even these were not being fulfilled.

Students were not being trained, informed or educated because they were not on campus long enough. The poorly prepared student or the student with average ability was being
flunked out. Academically talented students often transferred
after the second year. In the academic year 1954-55, only 262
students were enrolled in the fall, 212 students in the spring,
and 25 students graduated.

What was the financial situation? With an educational and
general budget of $239,906 in 1954-55, each student was cost-
ing the college $911 annually and contributing only $430 in
tuition and fees. Income from dormitories and other auxiliary
enterprises contributed only slightly more than the cost of their
operations. If student-teacher ratio was low, salaries were also
low; a devoted faculty was essentially subsidizing the college's
students.

The buildings were there; a faculty of 30 was there; a student body was not. An institution with few resources was offering a service for less than it was costing, and it could find few
students who would accept the offer. Neither the plant nor the
faculty was being used to capacity. An increase in income was
a necessity. Gifts were out of the question. The only visible
source for an increase in income was student fees.

Bold, clear-cut decisions had to be made. Whatever advantages there were in the situation had to be seized upon. The college had been living on new students whom it would ultimately flunk out. The first decision had to be made in terms of admissions.

It was decided that the actual admissions situation as it had existed for some years would be accepted, along with the responsibility that admission policy entailed. The college publicly announced this policy and has hewed to it. Substantially this policy is that approximately one-third of students admitted will come from the bottom half of high school classes. As was true in the past, students who had been unsuccessful in other colleges would be given a second chance.

Concomitant with this admission decision was the decision that every attempt would be made to fulfill the college's obligation in admitting these students. Special programs were set up for conditional and probational students. These programs will be discussed later.

With neither buildings nor faculty being used to capacity, it was possible to offer substantial scholarships to students who otherwise would not have been able to come to Parsons. Whatever portion of the normal tuition they paid added to income; their payments also added income to auxiliary enterprises—notably to income from sparsely occupied dormitories. Thus, in this initial phase, the increased number of scholarship students balanced the increased number of marginal students. The general increase in student body was the result of a vigorous admission campaign conducted on a national basis.

This was the first phase of the Parsons College experiment. With the exception of the resolution to fulfill the college's obligations to those marginal students admitted, no major changes in educational policies or methods were made. The college was brought toward financial stability by greater use of available facilities and available personnel.

A conscious attempt was made to hold the number of faculty members constant while the student body was doubling. Tuition, impossibly low in 1954-55, was raised. The student-teacher ratio went from 8.8 to 1 in 1954-55 to 15.6 to 1 in 1957-58. (The 1957-58 figures are necessarily approximate since some teachers were already being sent back to graduate school for advanced study at college expense.) By 1957-58 expenditures per student had gone down to $753 annually and tuition charges were $650—closer to a balance.

No significant additions were made to classroom space for several years. With increases in student body available space was used to the utmost. Classes were scheduled from eight until five in most rooms. Two-hour courses were eliminated and, for a while, Tuesday, Thursday, and Saturday classes were scheduled. However, student and faculty resistance to Saturday classes proved so intense that this schedule was unworkable. Instead three-hour classes were scheduled for an hour and a half Tuesday and Thursday.

In short, during this phase a pattern was set that resulted ultimately in a college that met all of its current expenses out of income from tuition, fees, and auxiliary enterprises. With no appreciable endowment, all future administrative decisions had to be made in terms that would not break the pattern of self-support set in the first years.

The major instructional developments of this first phase were the serious efforts made to restrain the drop out and flunk out of marginal students capable of doing college work. These efforts were of two kinds; intensified counseling and intensified teaching. The counseling and advisory program which provides for more structured and more frequent counseling than usual, varies little from many such programs and need not concern us here.

The workshop program with marginal students was significantly different. After the first six weeks, a student who fell below "C" in any course was scheduled into an extra session given by the professor in charge. He was also more closely supervised by his academic advisor. In the workshop special problems could be discussed and students drilled.

Later the professor was also expected to maintain office hours that made him available to students at any time during the day when he was not teaching. This availability was to allow for individual tutoring.

It becomes obvious at this point that with increased class size, increased number of advisory sessions, and added workshop and tutoring sessions, the work load of individual faculty members was prodigious. *The creation of a self-supporting college is directly dependent on the willingness of faculty members to concentrate upon teaching and to work harder at it than is normally expected.* It is this kind of concentration that has allowed faculty salaries to double and triple. Using the highest figure I could find, the median faculty salary at Parsons in 1954-55 was $3,400. The median is now well over $10,000.

The workshop-tutorial program at Parsons was directly dependent on the cooperation of the faculty, most of whom saw the necessity for a radical cut in the attrition rate. Though attempts were made to schedule workshops on the same basis as regular classes, no firmly structured situation could be worked out at first. Faculty had to make their own arrangements and it was some time before the workshop was considered a normal part of the life of the college. Often the students who needed it most failed to show up. This was even more true of attempts to get some kind of individual tutoring for the weakest students. The development of a fully structured program was still to come.

A real shift toward a greater academic emphasis began with tentative curriculum revision designed to create a set of core courses for all students regardless of major. This is not a new concept but was new to Parsons College. Characteristically, this began with various attempts to create science courses for non-science majors.

The most significant of the new required "core" courses was the experimental humanities or great books course begun in 1958. This was an attempt to provide a common core for *both* faculty and students. A one-hour course in humanities was to be required of all students throughout the four years, eight hours in all. Monthly an outside lecturer was brought in to talk on one of the books. Weekly students met in small sections to discuss the current book with a team of instructors. All faculty members were assigned to one or more sections. The faculty met monthly to discuss the current book and to go over specially prepared syllabus materials.

This course was significant for three reasons. First, no matter on how superficial a level, its aim was clearly to educate rather than train. It was designed to confront all the students with the perennial questions which in the end they must answer for themselves. Second, it was the first experiment in team teaching. Third, revision of the course had to be made largely because of faculty resistance.

I think it is understood that even where faculty members are hired into an experimental situation, they often tend to resist experiment. This is by no means irrational for college faculties are made up of men devoted to particular disciplines, men who have highly individuated views of how these disciplines should be communicated. Nonetheless, as David Reisman once indicated in a letter to Robert Jordan, college administrators tend to be more experimental minded than college faculties. In any experimental college a degree of faculty resistance must be expected.

In the case of the humanities program the team teaching method was new and members of the Humanities Division were uneasy. In other departments faculty members teaching outside their disciplines felt insecure and in some cases felt that their professional status was being undermined; in point of fact, some of the best teaching was done by members of the Science Division. This did not prevent cumulative faculty resistance from being one major factor in revision of the program. After one year only about half of the faculty was involved in teaching and after two years the course was revised into the normal three-hour pattern; after a short while it became the property of a separate department. Inter-disciplinary teaching and team teaching went by the boards but the idea of providing the student with a question-provoking core course was not lost.

Though a common core was in process of development, and in spite of administration attempts to discourage it, course proliferation continued. No analysis of the vested interests, individual and departmental, that tend to promote and maintain course proliferation is necessary here. Each of us as a teacher must have been responsible for adding at least one favorite course.

In spite of continued proliferation the college had grown increasingly prosperous. This prosperity had its own educational effect. It allowed the college to send a large number of faculty back to school to take further graduate work and thus increase competency. It also allowed a salary scale that, for the first time in some years, was competitive nationally. Thus better qualified teachers could be employed. Almost imperceptibly the goals the college had set itself were beginning to shift from a very large emphasis on training to greater emphasis on informing and educating the student. Training was not abandoned and, as the college grew in size, various additional training areas, largely appealing to young women, were added. But these were of no real importance and were gradually abandoned.

In the spring of 1960 the college decided to begin a trimester program the following summer. This trimester program speeded and ultimately facilitated all of the programs and experiments so far noted.

The trimester program created an almost ideal situation for the handling of marginal students. Applicants who were accepted conditionally were required to enter school in the summer trimester and were limited to twelve hours of academic work. Special programs could thus be arranged for them. Those who were found to be deficient in one area or another could be enrolled in special courses not counting toward graduation. Students already enrolled who had dropped below an acceptable academic average could be required to attend the summer trimester. Students who felt they were having difficulty could register for fewer hours and, by attending the summer trimester, still graduate within the normal four years.

It was thus possible to teach academically less talented students without placing excessive demands upon them and without flunking them out as long as they themselves were motivated to stay in school. A series of hurdles was created. A conditional student had to be motivated enough to enter in the summer. A probational student had to be motivated enough to spend summers in study. Rulings were made that no student was allowed to enter the upper division without a "C" average, but a student was permitted to retake courses to achieve this level. In most cases students who were not sufficiently motivated, or who had proved to themselves they were not capable of doing college work, flunked themselves out. There were some students, however, who, due to parental pressure or sheer unwillingness to enter work life, did persist. It was thus found necessary to place a limit on the number of trimesters a student could remain without achieving required averages. In general, however, the system of hurdles worked very well and inadequately motivated students eliminated themselves.

The trimester system required that, insofar as possible, all courses offered by the college be offered each trimester. As a consequence curriculum revision was a necessity. The faculty could easily see that the offering of an undue number of courses each trimester was an impossibility. The first cutback was from over 400 courses offered at that time to 160, including the 20 courses in the core. The 20 core courses were required of all students except those majoring in the sciences, who substituted science courses designed for majors. No course that was not a requirement for graduation in at least one departmental area was to be offered. With few exceptions, notably in the fine arts where additional courses are offered in the summers only, this line has been held.

Educationally, the effect of this change was to create a program that required all students to be at least informed in the liberal arts.

Under the system current in 1954-55 and persisting for some time thereafter, there were general college requirements of fifty-three hours (fifty-seven including physical education), many hours being elective: nineteen of these hours were in skill courses. In the new core of sixty hours, skill courses were held to eighteen hours and no hourly credit or grades were given for physical education.

Juniors and seniors who took a course outside their major field had to compete against majors in the field of that course. Even in major offerings, professors had to consider the educational needs of non-specialists. Again, the effect of the change was to weight the offerings toward informing and educating rather than simply training. Training, however, did persist and students with pure liberal arts majors accounted for only 36 per cent of upper division students in the spring trimester of 1962.

The trimester program was so structured that an appreciable

percentage of regularly enrolled students would attend the summer trimester. With the curriculum cutback a much higher percentage of the upper division courses could be offered than in the old type of short summer sessions. This attracted talented students who wished to graduate in two and two-thirds years. Inasmuch as all core courses could be offered, marginal students in the lower division were attracted, whether they were required to come or not, since, by attending the summer trimester they could, even if they cut back to an average of ten hours a trimester, graduate in four years. A summer arts festival in conjunction with increased offerings in the fields of the arts was designed to attract students in these areas; the festival helped make the summer pleasant for all in attendance. Students who attended summer sessions were offered a relatively inexpensive trimester abroad program. A work-study program was proposed.

Neither the trimester abroad program nor the work-study program attracted enough students to be worth continuing after the second year. The arts festival, however, was notably successful. In drama, for example, students were given the opportunity of performing with nationally known actors and actresses like Pat O'Brien, Faye Emerson, and Signe Hasso, all of whom proved more than willing to assist young people as well as to perform.

The result of this structuring was that enrollment in the summer was up to 77 per cent of enrollment in the fall, with a resultant 25 per cent increase in income. Costs for general administration, staff, library staff, and maintenance remained roughly constant. It was possible for some of the faculty who were teaching in the summer trimester to engage in further study or research during the fall or spring trimesters. Some faculty members, however, went on eleven-month contracts.

Here again is seen the principle of maximum use of plant and personnel resulting in a financially stable situation. The college was not only balancing its books but was beginning to show a surplus of income over expenditure. For the year 1962-63, including the prorated summer enrollment, the cost per student per trimester was $410; tuition and fees per trimester were set at $450. Thus in the educational and general budget alone there was a surplus.

The college could now afford the kind of faculty that could have only been dreamed of a few years before. With the appearance of this faculty the weight again was being shifted toward achievement of the strictly educational goal of the college. Richer resources were becoming available; for example, the book budget for the library was fifteen times that of 1954-55.

Testing procedures were being refined. Prospective students were required to present college board scores. After the first, fourth, and eighth semesters, all students are given the Graduate Record Examinations to keep track of their progress.

To many of us this seemed the time that the emphasis of the college could shift from training and informing our students to putting a great deal of weight on the process of making them think—or educating them. It seemed the time to structure such a change.

From my observation inside the classroom and in the library, the level of performance one could demand and get from students was very much higher than it had been when our experiment had begun. The difference in the papers being written in social science seminar, for example, was outstanding. It seemed the time for me, as librarian, to act. I was convinced that library techniques were the ideal method to educate. Within the library a student could be informed while being forced to find and select valid information, draw inferences, and weigh conclusions. In a library students could be taught to think.

To this end I conducted a campaign among faculty and administration that resulted in a program that was more than I had asked for. All upper division courses and selected courses in the core were to have term papers or equivalent library projects. Within limits the program was on the way toward accomplishing ideal educational goals.

Nevertheless, I had made a primary mistake. I had failed to take into consideration the kind of experiment in which I was participating. I had picked an ideal goal and ideal means with which to achieve it in a situation where I should have asked what *could* be done and then modified means to achieve this end. Realistically, having quickly sensed the problems, the program could have been modified to fit the situation. What was the situation? Having convinced deans and the faculty senate, I assumed the rest of the faculty agreed. I should have known from the writings of Patricia Knapp and Harvie Branscomb that the speculative or exploratory method of learning and teaching which is involved with library-oriented study is alien to most faculty members since their own training on the undergraduate level was not conducted in this way. Some faculty members, notably one professor of business, discovered that once they had tried teaching in this way that it was most successful. On the other hand, another very excellent professor scornfully dismissed the whole matter as a "progressive education idea."

Another major negative factor was the fact that, with a relatively high student-teacher ratio, the faculty was simply overloaded. Faced with a method of teaching of which some of them did not approve, papers were an extra burden—not a part of the teaching itself.

The program, modified over a few years, could have been worked out, for the college was wide open to all kinds of experiment; but some other faculty members made the same kind of mistake I made. A group of new men, coming into an experimental college, had envisioned ideal goals, ideal methods, and ideal students. Not understanding the situation as it once had been nor the improvements that had already been made, their disillusionment was almost absolute. Whatever their motives, the violence of their reaction was sufficiently confusing to convince me that it was the wrong time to push a program only half understood by a high percentage of the faculty.

Thus in view of my failure to consider carefully enough the nature of the experiment in which I was participating, the failure of some faculty members to understand the nature of library study, and the failure of a group of new faculty members to understand the nature of the college, the library way to improve education did not work out. It is a good way toward improved education and in time, given the continued atmosphere of experiment, it can become the Parsons College way.

But experiment had not stopped; the college was feeling its

way toward yet a different kind of program. A few courses were organized on a six-three-six basis: six weeks of class, three weeks out of class, and then six weeks in class. The three-week period was to be used for independent research papers, book reports or tutoring, depending on the level of the student. This program was found too unwieldy to be applied across the board. Faculty members would have been swamped with students needing special work during the three weeks and the library would have been swamped with students needing books. However, this idea of varying work for different kinds of students was combined with the earlier team teaching idea and the workshop idea, and a new approach made was to lower division teaching.

The new team teaching approach to the teaching of core courses combined most aspects of former experiments except the inter-disciplinary approach. The professor in charge of a course lectured to students three times a week. Associates, hired at first during the term paper program, met with small sections twice a week. Students dropping below "C" were encouraged to meet tutors at least once a week. The professor in charge kept office hours and was available for conferences with students.

Thus the team teaching idea, first seen in the humanities program, came into widespread use on the campus. The workshop idea was embodied in formally scheduled discussions sections. The hit-or-miss tutoring program now was staffed with young teachers whose only job was to tutor. All of the conventional teaching methods—lecture, discussion, and tutoring— were brought together in one package. Candidates for the master's degree were used in tutoring. Associates already had the master's and were working on the doctorate. In most cases, associates and tutors had at least one trimester off a year to work on their advanced degrees. Thus an in-service training program was developed—a program which had, in another form, sent a large number of teachers back to graduate school for advanced academic work.

Doubled contact hours for marginal students made the likelihood of their success that much greater. The marginal, conditional, or probational students could be placed in special discussion sections. The academically talented students could be put into honors sections. In this way the college's goal of training, informing, and educating students of all levels of ability could be accomplished with each group getting the kind of attention it needed. In the words of our current catalog, Parsons College now "provides a pattern which proposes to take each student from the place he stands on entering as far as patient and intensified teaching can develop his capabilities."

Thus hard headed, realistic experimentation has resulted in an institution which can realize the implicit goals of many small liberal arts colleges. The trimester system, maximum use of plant, maximum use of personnel, and astute handling of auxiliary enterprises has resulted in an institution which is viable and financially capable of competing with public institutions for faculty and staff. It can and does train, inform, and educate students of all levels of ability.

The Parsons College experiment is significant because it took place in a private institution whose educational and financial situation in 1955 was parallel to that of many private institutions in the United States. If the private liberal arts college is to continue to absorb an appreciable percentage of students currently seeking higher education, it must find educational methods that will fit our new situations, nationally and internationally. It must find the financial ways to compete for adequate faculty and provide adequate resources.

Failures of some experiments and consequent revisions are as significant to study as are our successes. For some period the college's attempt to cut back curriculum and stop course proliferation met with failure due to the natural desires of departments and individual faculty members. However, on reorganization in terms of a trimester program, the necessity for such cutbacks could be clearly seen and the curriculum was revised and cut back in a short period. When the attempt was made to combine team teaching methods with inter-disciplinary teaching in the humanities program, resistance was met on all sides and the program had to be revised. However, when team teaching was applied by the departments to core courses and adapted to them, team teaching was successful. The experimental, nonstructured workshop program, though it was effective to a considerable degree, was dependent upon the cooperation of individuals. Incorporated into the structure of team teaching of core courses, the workshop principle was easily applied since the program made for opportunities for the academically talented as well as for the academically marginal student. The term paper program applied to all upper division courses involved a major change in teaching methods and was essentially dependent upon individual cooperation and was not successful. A method of applying library teaching methods on a school-wide basis is still to be worked out.

These necessary modifications would indicate that the following things are necessary if experimentation is to be successful. A change of teaching method, to be successful, should not be combined with any other change. In short, one thing at a time. Second, successful changes in curriculum or method can best be made when there is a clear and pressing reason for these changes. Examples of this may be seen in the curriculum cuts made at the time of initiating the trimester program and in the establishment of the workshop program when it was apparent attrition rates must be cut. Any change in a college program of a major sort should, for best results, not depend completely upon the cooperation of individuals as individuals. However, essential to any experimentation is the clear understanding, and at best, the agreement of individuals. Successful experimentation is ultimately dependent upon the devotion and teaching competence of the college's faculty as a whole. This devotion, however, must be channeled into appropriate organized programs.

The specific contribution of Parsons College's successful experimentation is the demonstration that small institutions with small physical plants and small faculties can expand their student bodies and, far from losing educational effectiveness and financial stability, can gain on both counts. With college population now coming to a new peak, many private colleges can use the Parsons experiment as a guide if their decision is to expand. Proper scheduling of classroom space combined with cutbacks in the number of course offerings can provide for a sensible program to be offered to increased numbers of students. The fact that one sample study of 200 of our graduates during the expansion period shows that 35 per cent went on to graduate school demonstrates the fact that educational effectiveness need not be lost even in the confusion of expansion. The Parsons College experiment also indicates that it is possible to absorb poorly trained students or students of marginal ability and train them effectively. The degree of waste which is resulting from flunk-out policies in many institutions of higher education is indicated by the high degree of success Parsons College has had with transfer students. A study of a sample of 200 students enrolled in the spring trimester 1962, each of whom had transferred into Parsons with a cumulative average below "C", showed over 70 per cent had a "C" average or better during that semester. An estimated 80 per cent could ultimately be expected to achieve satisfactory performance.

Parsons has demonstrated that a year-round college can be valuable for both marginal students and students of exceptional ability. It has demonstrated that a trimester system, rather than being a financial liability can be a financial asset, if the trimester program is properly structured to appeal to a high percentage of normal enrollment during a summer trimester. The over-all results of this series of Parsons experiments shows that the private, unendowed liberal arts college can be made into a financially viable institution and need not depend on private donors or government appropriations. The situation is now such that, using Parsons' methods, private colleges with very different admissions policies can compete for competent staff and continue to play a major role in higher education.

Since 1960 the educational and general budget at Parsons College has been met by student payments of tuition and fees. Until that time deficits were made up by profitable operation of auxiliary enterprises—a subsidy built into the operation. Such excess of income over expenditure from room, board, bookstore, and student union can now be devoted to capital expenditures. Planned or completed are a new library and science complex, a social science building, a humanities building, improved library collections, a student center, and new dormitories. This building program is projected for amortization in the next five years.

The experiment continues.

Chapter 6

THE UNIVERSITY OF THE PACIFIC AND ITS "CLUSTER COLLEGES"

By SAMUEL L. MEYER*

The University as a Whole

The University of the Pacific is California's first chartered institution of higher learning. It was established by action of an educational conference of Methodist leaders which met in San Jose on January 6 and 7, 1851. The University was chartered by the Supreme Court of California on July 10, 1851, as California Wesleyan College. In 1852 the name was changed to the University of the Pacific. The institution operated under that name until 1911 when it became the College of the Pacific. The Pacific Conservatory of Music, the first of its professional schools, was organized in 1878. A School of Education was established in 1924. After long consideration, the College was moved in 1924 from San Jose to Stockton in the fabulous San Joaquin Valley near the geographical center of the state of California.

Since the Second World War the University of the Pacific has expanded rapidly—physically, financially, and academically. From 1935 to 1951, the College of the Pacific restricted its offerings to junior, senior, and graduate studies a coordinated operation with the publicly supported Stockton College which offered freshman and sophomore courses. In the latter year (1951) Pacific reinstated its own lower division work when Stockton College, now known as San Joaquin Delta College, moved to its own campus. A School of Pharmacy was organized at Pacific in 1955. A Division of Graduate Studies, known since 1961 as the Graduate School, was recognized in 1956. The

*Mr. Meyer is Academic Vice President, University of the Pacific, Stockton, California.

73

School of Engineering opened in 1957. As a result of these developments it became obvious that the name College of the Pacific was a misnomer so, on Founder's Day, January 6, 1961, the institution returned to its earlier name, the University of the Pacific.

In 1962 the College of Physicians and Surgeons, a school of dentistry founded in San Francisco in 1896, became an integral part of the University of the Pacific. In 1962, also, the administrative structure of the College of Liberal Arts was formalized and a dean was appointed. Under the designation, "The College of the Pacific," it preserves the earlier name used by the total institution, a name abbreviated to and used affectionately by many as "COP."

In this way, through more than 113 years, a small, regional, church related, liberal arts college has been transformed into a medium-sized, multi-purposed, church related university of national and international significance.

The University and California Higher Education

It is toward the more recent developments in the life of the University of the Pacific that we should now direct our attention.

It was in the Summer of 1958 that President Robert E. Burns and those associated with him in the leadership of the University of the Pacific sat down together and looked into the future of private higher education in California. The prospects were not encouraging. About them was a complex of publicly-supported institutions of higher learning, the extent of which is almost incomprehensible to persons outside California. This was the system which was to bring together in the fall of 1964 some 64,500 students on the eight campuses and related facilities of the University of California, more than 133,100 students in 16 state colleges, and something over 368,000 students in junior colleges on 91 campuses in 63 junior college districts. This represents a publicly-supported educational colossus of more than 565,000 students above the high school level. Behind it are the tremendous financial resources of the most rapidly growing state in the nation.

What was Pacific to do? Should it grow larger and sacrifice

those values which had characterized its educational process for more than 100 years: small classes, intimate personal student-faculty relationships, individual counseling and guidance, a campus residence experience, participation in a community of learning where each member is important, opportunity for exploration and experimentation, emphasis on moral and spiritual values, academic freedom? Should we hold our own and become a voice of ever-decreasing consequence in the challenging future of California higher education? Neither of these alternatives appealed to Pacific's leadership that summer day in 1958.

The "Cluster College" Concept

It was President Burns who made a courageous and pioneering decision. He said:

> Let us grow larger by growing smaller. Let us develop about the University a cluster of colleges which will retain the values we cherish so much and, yet, will, at the same time, make it possible for us to accept some responsibility for educating the increasing number of young people seeking to enter institutions of higher learning in California. Let us follow the Oxford and Cambridge system and expand by establishing small, interrelated colleges clustered together to draw strength from each other and from the University as a whole.

Thus, the "cluster college" concept of the University of the Pacific came into being.

Some guide lines were laid down for the development of the new colleges. Each was to be small with a maximum enrollment of 250 students. Each was to have its own faculty and chief administrative officer to be designated by an appropriate title such as provost, director, rector, or dean. Each was to be residential with emphasis on "living and learning" together. The physical arrangement of the buildings for each college, using the quadrangle plan, would foster the close faculty student relationships which lie at the very heart of the learning process. The students in each of the colleges would not only enjoy the graciousness of living in a beautiful setting but would, also, be able to carry the intellectual stimulation and searching that excites them in the classroom into the dining hall where they sit down together for meals, into the common room or social hall where they meet informally with each other or with their professors, and on into their dormitory lounges and rooms. Each college was to develop its own traditions and distinctive character. The faculty of each college was to enjoy sufficient autonomy and freedom in curriculum building to produce a different academic flavor and to introduce all manner of teaching innovations. It was expected, however, that the academic program of each of the colleges, so far as could then be determined, would be liberal arts centered.

At the same time each college was to be very much a part of the total University. All would have the same board of regents, president, academic vice-president, and other chief administrative officers. Essential services were to be provided each of the colleges by the business office, admissions office, registrar's office, and the public relations and development offices of the University. Although each college was to have its own dormitories, dining halls, lounges and social halls, administrative and faculty offices, it would use, for the most part, the library, classroom, laboratory, athletic, and health service facilities on the main campus. Students in the "cluster colleges" would be represented in the Pacific Student Association and would be eligible to hold student body offices. They might participate in the varied extra-curricular activities of the University such as drama, debate, intercollegiate athletics, band, orchestra, and choir. Students from all the colleges were to receive degrees conferred by the University. "Cluster college" faculty members were to be full members of the University faculty community and might be called upon to serve on appropriate University committees. Since it was expected that all of the colleges would be undergraduate in scope, "cluster college" faculty members might, from time to time and as the scheduling of classes in their own colleges permitted, find it possible to teach graduate courses and seminars, to serve on graduate committees, and even to direct the study of graduate students working within the various areas of the University in which post-baccalaureate programs were available.

Raymond College

Raymond College, the first of the series of colleges to be clustered about the parent institution, accepted its first class in September, 1962. The College was named for Mr. and Mrs. Walter Raymond of Knight's Landing, California, whose beneficence brought this dream of academic excellence and innovation into being.

The opening of Raymond College was preceded by a long period of planning and building which included visits to Oxford and Cambridge universities in England. During study tours at those old and distinguished institutions of learning Pacific's administrators "lived in" at some of the colleges; met professors and tutors; talked with students; ate in great halls; visited tutorials, lectures, laboratories, and libraries; and observed and absorbed something of the traditions of the institutions.

It was, from the very start, a part of our thinking that the first of the "cluster colleges" should be a liberal arts college but that it should differ in important ways from other such colleges. Among the point of difference would be these:

1. The curriculum would be as free from professional orientation as possible. The emphasis would be more on education, less on training; more on the acquisition of knowledge, less on learning skills.

2. The curriculum would be limited. We asked ourselves these questions: What do we want to see happen to students between the time they enter and the time they leave Raymond College? How can we judge what is happening? What kind of experiences will be called for to make sure that certain things do happen? How do these experiences reflect themselves in the curriculum?

3. The curriculum was to indicate the unity rather than the compartmentalization of knowledge. In Raymond College there were to be no "departments" with their vested interests and historic records of vying for position and influence.

4. The curriculum was to place emphasis on the interdisciplinary concepts with the resulting cross-fertilization and stimulation of ideas.

5. The teaching method would make use of the seminar and the tutorial, the confrontation of teacher and student in the exchange of ideas and the stretching of the mind.

6. Within the academic structure of the new college the emphasis was to be on *learning* rather than on *teaching*. There is a vital difference.

7. We planned to make every effort to reduce the non-teaching duties of the faculty. It was our feeling that many, probably most, college teachers are diverted from their primary function by a wide variety of non-teaching duties. Some of these duties are both important and necessary; others are neither important nor necessary. In the small community in which Raymond students would live and learn, the faculty could share those responsibilities and find ways of working at the highest and most productive levels.

8. Starting with what we had and with the autonomy which had been granted to it, we hoped the Raymond faculty would resist the tendency to proliferate the curriculum. We knew it was not perfect. After all, men had made it but we felt it would be most unwise to introduce new courses representative of narrow specialties. At its very first meeting we urged the Raymond faculty, when thinking of revising the curriculum, to ask themselves these questions: In this field, what does a student *really* need to know? Does the lack of a specific course in this area *really* mean a loss in educational service? Is there no independent learning outside the structure of a formal course?

9. It was our feeling that the new college should not be bound by the traditions of the past. We felt its leadership and faculty must be freed of the limitations and restrictions developed on the campus of an institution as old as the University of the Pacific. We felt its faculty must be free to choose, to test, to evaluate, to produce.

Raymond College is now in its second year. In the words of its Provost, Warren B. Martin, "The Raymond Program is focused on participation in cooperative group endeavors and on individual academic adventures. The organization of the curriculum reflects the confidence of the College that motivated, disciplined students can, should, and will participate actively in their own education."

The student entering Raymond accepts a curriculum that emphasizes the classical divisions of the liberal arts—the humanities, the social sciences, and the natural sciences. While some variation in emphasis is possible, the Raymond Program, basically speaking, provides a curriculum that is uniform for all. It should not be supposed that such a curriculum makes no provision for special interests or individual abilities. Within the broad requirements of the several courses in the three divisions there is considerable latitude for individual specialization and concentration. The academic needs of the student within specific study areas are sought out, respected, and given a full range of development under tutorial guidance.

At Raymond College the student is challenged to do his work *faster* and *better*.

He works *faster* because:

1. He takes three terms of work each academic year. Each term is twelve to thirteen weeks in length, somewhat longer than the traditional quarter and somewhat shorter than the traditional semester. Each term provides 62 or 63 class meetings.

2. He takes three courses each term. Each course may meet as much as five hours per week and each "hour" is a full sixty minutes. With five meeting periods of sixty minutes each per week, each term at Raymond has the weight of a semester. There is not less than a thirty-minute "break" scheduled between one "hour'" and the next so that, if an exciting discussion gets going in one class, it is not necessary to bring it to a halt so that students can get to the next class within the ten minutes usually allotted.

3. At the end of three years or nine terms the Raymond student may have accumulated as many as 135 semester hour equivalents and is graduated with the degree of Bachelor of Arts.

He works *better* because:

1. The curriculum has been planned to provide opportunity for study in depth.

2. The instructional methodology features seminars, tuto-

rials, independent and directed study in an academic community in which a faculty-student ratio of 1:10 is maintained.

3. The physical plan of the college facilities with residence houses, faculty offices, seminar rooms, science laboratory, the Common Room with its library, the multi-purpose Great Hall, the Provost's Lodge, and some faculty apartments all within close proximity to each other makes it possible to relate "living and learning" in a unique way.

4. With a carefully selected student body limited to 250 and with all students required to "live in," the lives of Raymond students are oriented to learning and to the advantages to be achieved through active participation in a community of scholars.

In the freshman year the Raymond student studies French, German, Spanish, or Latin for three terms, with the second and third terms emphasizing readings in the literature of the language; one term of written and oral English; two terms of Math Analysis or one term of Math Analysis and one term of Physics; one term of Introduction to the Modern World (History); and two terms of seminar in either Readings in World Civilization or Readings in World Literature. At the end of the first year all students take their pre-Intermediate examinations. These are written examinations in each of the areas of the first year program—language, mathematics, literature or history. On these tests and in his course requirements the student must demonstrate the necessary proficiency to qualify for Intermediate standing. Aside from evaluation of the tests just mentioned and a regular term letter—a written statement indicating the student's accomplishment in the course, his areas of strength and weakness, and other observations based on the formal and informal association between student and teacher and sent to students and parents at the end of each term—the Raymond student works without formal, scheduled examinations until he reaches the third term of his senior year.

The Intermediate year student will spend his first and second terms in the seminar in Readings in World Civilization or Readings in World Literature, followed by a term of independent study in the area not followed in the three-term sequence just completed; a term of Physics or Chemistry; a term of Chemistry or Biology; a term of Biology, Advanced Mathematics, or science specialization; and a term in The Humanistic Tradition, with term emphases on fine arts, philosophy, and religion.

The Raymond College senior will take a three-term seminar in The Person and Modern Society, with term emphases in psychology, sociology, and economics. He will take a series of three seminars: Readings in United States History, Problems in American Democracy (Political Science), and Readings in American Civilization. In this year, also, he will take either a tutorial for each of the three terms in some area of specialization or 6 to 12 units in courses offered elsewhere in the University. In the spring term of this year he will be expected to take his comprehensive examinations. These consist of a written examination in each of the divisions of the curriculum—the humanities, the social sciences, and the natural sciences—and a public oral examination before representatives of the Raymond faculty and their "visitors" (professors from other colleges). Questions in the oral examination may probe the student's preparation in any of the three divisions of the curriculum and the area of his concentration or special study.

Graduating in three years, the Raymond student is prepared, if he so desires, to enter graduate school at the fourth year out of high school. If the student plans to enter some field that requires additional, specific training not included in the Raymond curriculum, he is free to concentrate on the courses he will need in this or some other institution. Since the Raymond curriculum is sufficiently flexible in the third year to permit some concentration in all three terms, it is expected that the student can usually proceed directly into graduate school. For most professions the Raymond Program is an ideal undergraduate preparation. It is certainly of great value for all those who desire a sound liberal arts education as an introduction to the finest aspects of our civilization.

To quote Provost Martin once again, Raymond College provides "a significant answer to the needs of the time. It is a thrilling concept, a venturesome idea, an exciting innovation that should not only benefit the student of today but be a source of pride and interested concern for the student of yesterday as he or she watches the program unfold and, in years to come, has an opportunity to observe the outstanding young men and women who will emerge."

Elbert Covell College

At a faculty retreat held in Columbia, California, on February 12, 1959, the attention of the faculty and staff of what was then the College of the Pacific was called to the possibility of developing a program of inter-American studies as a contribution to international understanding.

There were many reasons for this. The state of California has close historic ties with Mexico; a high proportion of the population of the state is Spanish-speaking; the Methodist Church, to which the University of the Pacific is related, has long been involved in an extensive missionary and educational program in Central and South America; the College was already committed to studies in California History and Western Americana; the most advanced techniques and equipment for the teaching of foreign languages, including Spanish, are used; for a small college with a small faculty, a surprisingly large number of faculty members were already bilingual in English and Spanish and had close personal and professional ties with Latin America. With such resources it was felt that the College of the Pacific could make an important contribution in this significant field.

Before making definite plans it was decided that representatives of Pacific should go to South America and obtain at first hand the information which would be needed before such a program could be proposed. During the summer of 1960 Pacific's president and academic vice-president visited South America, traveled thousands of miles in ten countries, and talked with hundreds of people in all walks of life. They did not go to tell the people what Pacific was going to do; rather, they went to seek information and to get ideas. They visited Panama, Colombia, Ecuador, Peru, Chile, Argentina, Uruguay, Paraguay, Brazil, and Venezuela. They talked with educators, businessmen, editors, embassy staff members, ambassadors, officials of the binational centers, representatives of various agencies such as the Fulbright Commission and the Rockefeller Foundation, and others from whom valuable information was obtained.

In Caracas, on their way back to California, Pacific's president and academic vice-president organized their voluminous notes, ideas, and suggestions and constructed a program of inter-American studies.

The first public announcement of this program was made at the 110th Founder's Day Convocation, held on January 6, 1961, when the name of the institution was changed back to University of the Pacific. One item in the "twelve point program" presented on that historic occasion was this: "As the 'Oxford type' cluster colleges to be associated with the University of the Pacific develop, to consider the possibility of designating one of the colleges, perhaps the second to be founded, as a liberal arts college in which all instruction will be in the Spanish language, an academic innovation of major significance."

The idea for a Spanish-speaking college in North America had arisen from a conversation among Pacific's president, academic vice-president, and Ambassador Robert F. Woodward, then United States Ambassador to Uruguay, in his home in Montevideo when the three men were discussing the problems facing Latin American students when they come to the United States for a college-level education. It was the ambassador's opinion that the greatest obstacle facing such students was the language barrier, all too often an insurmountable deterrent to satisfactory academic progress.

Since that day in 1960 much progress has been made. A benefactor, Mr. Elbert Covell of Woodbridge, California, and a member of the University's Board of Regents, who in February, 1964, celebrated his ninetieth birthday, came forward. His interest, dedication, and generosity made possible the establishment of the Spanish-speaking college which now bears his name, a project which is unique to education in the United States since it offers the first collegiate degree program ever made available in a language other than English. The physical plant consisting of three dormitories, a dining hall, "El Centro Administrativo," and "El Patio"—the social hall and lounge—have been completed and occupied. A highly competent bilingual faculty has been assembled. Classes began on September 4, 1963, for 59 Latin American and North American students representing 12 Latin American countries and the United States. The Latin American countries represented by this first student group were: Argentina, Bolivia, Chile, Colombia, the Dominican Republic, El Salvador, Guatemala, Honduras, Mexico, Nicaragua, Paraguay, and Peru. The curriculum and calendar are synchronized with those of the College of Pacific and the professional schools on the Stockton campus. All courses are taught in Spanish with the exception of English which, in Elbert Covell College, is taught as a foreign language. A total enrollment of 250 students is planned. Arthur J. Cullen, the Director of the College, came to the University in 1961 from Puerto Rico and has brought outstanding insight, experience, and leadership. Elliott J. Taylor, Pacific's dean of admissions, has extended his student recruitment tours to include Latin America in 1963 and 1964. A collection of several thousand volumes, known as the "Coleccion Presidente Adolpho Lopez Mateos," has been presented to the library by the Mexican government and various cultural institutions of Mexico. The Argentine Ministry of Education has contributed over two hundred books to the library. Gift books from Rotary clubs throughout Latin America are being collected by the North Stockton Rotary Club. A gift of flags representing 21 American Republics and Spain has been donated by the San Francisco Chapter of the Pan American Society. These now hang in the Elbert Covell College dining hall. Thus, the second of Pacific's "cluster colleges" is on the way.

Something of the significance of this step taken by the University of the Pacific can be appreciated when one reads two letters addressed to President Robert E. Burns.

One letter came from Ramon Menendez Pidal, then 92 years of age and President of the Spanish Royal Academy, and was dated May 29, 1962, in Madrid. He wrote, in translation:

> Greetings to Elbert Covell College—effusive greetings because of the innovation of the College in giving the years of instruction in Spanish by using that language exclusively in conducting all studies. I send, with my greetings, my confident hopes for the results which will be achieved by Elbert

Covell College in bringing about more intimate mutual understanding between the people of the two great languages most extensively used in the Americas.

The second letter came from the late President John F. Kennedy and is dated at the White House on June 8, 1962. It reads:

I send my warmest congratulations to the President, the Regents, the Faculty, and all the students of the University of the Pacific on the occasion of the establishment of the Elbert Covell College. This new college which, I understand, will offer four years of academic courses, all taught entirely in the Spanish language, opens up new vistas of enlightened international relationships between the people of the United States and the 16 million or more people in 19 Spanish-speaking nations.

The cause of peace which we are pursuing in the Alliance for Progress, requires the intimate understanding and the ability to communicate which are enhanced immeasurably by expert knowledge of this great language. Moreover, the student who can explore the wealth of culture, art, history, and human experience, which is recorded in the Spanish language, can greatly enrich the lives of his fellow citizens in our own country.

President Kennedy's concluding paragraph expressed a thought which a cruel fate decided was one in which he would not participate when he wrote, "We shall all look forward to watching the progress of Elbert Covell College, and I am confident that, in a few short years, we shall be hearing much of the achievements of its graduates."

The objectives of the Elbert Covell College are:

1. To train men and women as "inter-American specialists."

2. To give Latin American students the opportunity for a quality education and technical knowledge acquired in their own language, thus freeing them of the problem of learning language and subject matter at the same time, the barrier faced by foreign students in other institutions of collegiate grade in the United States.

3. To give North American students the opportunity for superior training in inter-American studies where the program has been carefully tailored to meet current needs.

4. To make it possible for Latin American students, if they so choose and if their competency in the language permits, to move out into the English-speaking curricula of the University for a part of their academic work.

5. To give students from all the Americas the opportunity to live and study together; to represent well their respective cultures to each other; and to accept the responsibility of learning to understand each other better.

6. To make available, within the framework of a truly inter-American concept, the historic values of a North American liberal arts education.

Director Cullen has defined the "inter-American specialist" in these terms:

> He must be, first of all, a specialist in one of the critical needs of the Americas. He completes a major of sufficient breadth and depth to allow him to pursue graduate work toward an advanced degree in his subject matter area or in a professional field related to it. The inter-American specialist is bilingual. He understands, speaks, reads and writes both the English and Spanish languages sufficiently well to communicate professionally and socially. The inter-American specialist has been well grounded in "area" courses; he knows the history, the forms of government, the literature, the art, the music, the traditions, the economic problems, the way-of-life of his own people, as well as those of the other America. The traditional Latin American studies program becomes only a part of his training, equal in importance to—but of questionable value unless accompanied by—language skills and professional competence.

At Elbert Covell College, a curriculum has been constructed and a faculty assembled to meet three critical needs of the Americas in the Twentieth Century: science and mathematics, business administration and economics, and teacher education. A "cluster college" with excellent physical facilities and a fine faculty, located in the center of a University with schools of pharmacy, dentistry, education, music, engineering, and liberal arts, Elbert Covell College commits all its offerings and pervades those of the entire University for the benefit of all the Americas. Faculty, library resources, classrooms, laboratories, equipment, scholarships, and services for a self-contained educational community that is truly "unique" by any standards known to North American higher education are being provided by Elbert Covell College so that this significant contribution to inter-American relations can fulfill its worthy objectives.

St. Michael's College

On October 17, 1963, the University of the Pacific announced that the Eighth Province of the Episcopal Church will establish St. Michael's College as a part of its "cluster college" pattern.

St. Michael's will be the only Episcopal college west of the Mississippi River. It will be an autonomous, undergraduate, liberal arts college, possibly oriented toward an academic emphasis on the humanities, which will differ somewhat in its relations to the University from the "cluster colleges" which are brought into being by the University itself. For example, it has its own board of trustees, it will be responsible for its own financing, and it may ultimately have as many as 750 to 800 students. A site will be provided by the University on a long-term lease basis. On the other hand, St. Michael's will use the University's laboratories, library, athletic fields, infirmary, and other general facilities. All students of this College will be considered students of the University as is true also of students in Raymond College and Covell College. St. Michael's College faculty members will be faculty members of the University. Academically, St. Michael's College will be responsible to the University of the Pacific in whose name the degrees will be conferred.

The Board of Trustees of St. Michael's has been named and has held a number of meetings. Plans for buildings and curriculum, both to be created within the Angelican ethos, are progressing. It is now expected that St. Michael's College will open not later than 1967.

Other "Cluster Colleges"

Construction has recently begun on the dormitories, dining room, and social hall for yet another college which will complete a planned physical relationship to Raymond and Covell as a result of which the food services for the three college quad-rangles will come from the same kitchen. Drawings are being prepared for an academic facilities building which will serve the same three colleges. The expanding program of "cluster colleges" calls for a new science building and an addition to the University library, all to be completed prior to 1968.

At present there are no definite plans for the distinctive ob-jectives and curriculum of the college now under construction. These await our imagination and initiative. Until such time as they are developed, the available space will be used by students in other divisions of the University. It is sufficient to say that by 1976, the year in which the 125th anniversary of the found-ing of the University of the Pacific will be observed, there will be four "cluster colleges" in addition to Raymond, Covell, and St. Michael's.

Concluding Comments

Half facetiously and half seriously referred to as "Oxford on the Calaveras," national attention is focused on the University of the Pacific where private higher education is trying to meet the challenge of the times in a somewhat different way.

In the May, 1962, issue of *Liberal Education*, official bulle-tin of the Association of American Colleges, F. L. Wormald, the editor, included among his "Editorial Notes," this com-ment:

> The Oxbridge pattern of University organization seems to be peculiarly attractive to California colleges. Following the Claremont group but apparently coming even closer to the English model, the University of the Pacific at Stockton is developing what it calls a "cluster college system." Two col-leges, each of which will have its own dormitories, dining hall, classrooms and faculty, and will be limited to 250 stu-dents, are already under construction. A unique feature of the plan is that one of the colleges, Elbert Covell, will offer 150 students from Latin America and 100 Norteamericanos a complete program in the liberal arts taught entirely in Spanish. We have often been inclined to boast that our own alma mater stands high in the ranks of truly international institutions but in at least one respect it must yield pride of place to the University of the Pacific.

More recently, in the September 30, 1963, issue of *Newsweek*, under the heading, "Total Immersion," there was a two-column story about Pacific with detailed emphasis on the program of Elbert Covell College and general reference to Pacific's plan to grow by adding " 'cluster colleges,' each with a distinctive education approach."

That attention continues to be focused on Pacific is further illustrated by the fact that the October 11, 1963, issue of *Time* magazine carried a story about the University under the title, "Reform on the Coast." The *Time* writer concluded his article with the prophecy that, "Pacific may become one of the nation's most interesting campuses."

"Growing larger by growing smaller," the "sharpening of the mind" within the small college atmosphere where every student has a "feeling of belonging," is the concept which will permit the University of the Pacific to accept its fair share of the rapidly growing numbers of college-bound youth and, at the same time, retain all of the best features and advantages of the small, private, church related institution of higher learning.

Chapter 7

FLORIDA PRESBYTERIAN COLLEGE:
NEW ADVENTURE IN EDUCATION

By John M. Bevan*

Florida Presbyterian College is located in St. Petersburg, Florida. It was chartered in 1958 as a coeducational, residential, liberal arts college under the joint sponsorship of the Florida Synods of both the Presbyterian Church in the United States and the United Presbyterian Church in the United States of America. Feasibility studies were conducted in 1955-1957; the Board of Trustees was appointed in February of 1958, the President selected in June of the same year and the Dean of Faculty in February of 1959; the first faculty of 22 was assembled by November of 1959 and the first freshman class of 150 was in residence in September of 1960. From 1960 to 1962 classes were conducted on an interim campus and were transferred to the permanent campus in September of 1962. This campus is a 290-acre site on Boca Ciega Bay. The campus plan calls for an $18,000,000 physical plant and to date construction in the amount of $8,000,000 has been completed. At present the student body numbers 700, the faculty 56 and projections in this category estimate by 1970 a maximum enrollment of 1,500 and a faculty of 75. Seventy-two students were awarded degrees in June of 1964.

The Perspective

To meet the needs of both a faculty and a student body who are mutually involved in the pursuit of learning, the program at Florida Presbyterian College was designed and executed so as to provide: (1) an orientation that maintains the independence and interdependence of all academic disciplines, (2) depth and breadth of intellectual experience, (3) an opportunity to extend one's capacities and efforts through corporate and in-

*Mr. Bevan is Dean of the College, Florida Presbyterian College, St. Petersburg, Florida.

dependent study in the direction and to the limits desired, (4) continued stimulation that facilitates mental, moral, and physical growth, and (5) the engenderment of a wholesome and critical enthusiasm for inquiry and reflection that will extend beyond the period of formal education. It has been recognized, furthermore, that such a program must be defined in a manner that makes it economically feasible, elastic, and reasonably exhaustive. Too, it is unmistakably clear that any plan for general education which seeks to fulfill such ends can never be final or perfect and that modifications will always be necessary so as to keep abreast with new departures in areas of study and methods of teaching. What is programed at any moment must be considered now and later as tentative in the sense that present and future experiences primarily guide and direct toward the goals conceived.

In elaborating the curriculum or modus operandi for such a program several problems basic to education today were examined; namely, independent study, the unification of knowledge, separations within the academic community, the place of values, a student's involvement in the learning of another student, economics, and continuing education. Too, projections as to future trends which may gain eminency as the result of contemporary research and conditions played an equally vital role. (What happens when indicators point out the possibility of an almost revolutionary and inevitable redefinition of the elementary, junior high, and senior high school programs which develop the average child to the place that he reads certain works at a rate of 1,500 to 2,000 words per minute, speaks well two foreign languages, has become somewhat proficient in independent study as the result of a carefully guided process that began in seventh grade and culminated in contract study and research in the advanced grades? Is it so ridiculous and farfetched now to assume that within the next twenty-five years we shall witness the introduction at the third and fourth grade levels of a formal reading program making use of shadowscopes and rate pacers, the expansion of the foreign language program beginning at the same level, the redefinition of the junior high years as a transition period between the more formal instruction of the elementary level and the independent study programs of senior high where formal classroom instruction has given way to procedures through which students independently contract their assignments with a teacher who seldom lectures but who is almost always available to answer questions and give needed guidance in study?) The many new insights growing out of our research and the demands of our times make innovation a necessity. Add to this the facts that we cannot train fast enough the number of teachers needed, build school buildings at the rate commensurate with school population growth, and in the age of the atomic bomb find monies sufficient to do what must be done to maintain the present structure and quality of our educational program. It may be that our present day program of education in these United States of America is fast becoming outmoded and must undergo a metamorphosis or suffer the crippling effects of old age.

With these objectives, trends, and conditions in mind, a curriculum was designed which would serve the college constituency of the moment (i.e., it would not frighten the prospective student and his parents), yet would be easily re-shaped to allow innovations as trends dictated (i.e., a "sixty per cent" independent study program in which the library gains the central focus we have so long contended it has held; elimination for the most part of the textbook-survey approach and its course-semester structure with its laborious point-credit and cut systems that tend to give education its terminal attitude and status and make unavailable to the student many exciting learning experiences the curriculum offers; a mass lecture-seminar structure which allows more frequent and intensive disputation and conceivably is more economical; an exchange between academic disciplines heretofore confined primarily to a particular division but seldom experienced beyond division barriers and without depriving the professor participating of time for continued growth and recognition within its own discipline; and so on).

As already has been indicated great emphasis is being given at Florida Presbyterian College to independent study in the hope of evolving the kind of program alluded to earlier. What follows in this report is a brief summary of the reflections on and development in this area of curriculum planning.

Development of Independent Study Program

Too frequently the teacher stands in a place similar to the mule driver who has had animals equipped with blinders as he holds tight to the reins and cracks his whip about the animals' ears. Similarly, in the classroom freedom and latitude in self-expression are usually discouraged and education is presented as a fiat. To be sure many such situations are enhanced in their rigor by pop quizzes and the like but they seldom produce greater self insight, inspire personal initiative, or develop acceptance of responsibility. Instead of encouragement and personal challenge in placing more responsibility on the student for his own education the teacher defines the situation in its totality, motivates the subject by all sorts of neurotic devices designed to make learning something from which to escape, establishes as a goal the grade, and then points his finger of scorn at the student accusing him of being immature, unresourceful and only slightly interested in learning. (It is nothing short of a miracle that out of such an authoritative atmosphere individuals do emerge who are mature, imaginative, and creative.)

A note of encouragement in this situation comes from the more recent multiplication of programs and explorations in independent study, a modus vivendi in which primary initiative for learning belongs with the student. Conclusions drawn from research in these programs indicate that opportunity for initial exposure to independent study should be present in the first year of college, if not before; that such programs should be expanded to involve more of the student population; that orientation programs designed to incite appropriate attitudes of independent study are of little avail; that learning in independent study, as evidenced by test performance is neither better nor worse than that demonstrated in groups studying under conventional methods; that the primary key to effective independent study programs is a nucleus of faculty who "accepts at face value" the student's presumed interest in learning how to learn by himself; that economic benefits may accrue in an institution where independent study becomes an "academic way of life."

One of the primary aims at Florida Presbyterian College is

to develop a program in which independent study might become an academic way of life. In the evolution of such a college atmosphere the following *conditions* were initiated and the following *procedures* were pursued:

1. Admittance to the college of better than average students only for no other reason than it might make the initial experimentation easier.

2. Selection of a highly competent faculty, each member being decidedly interested in experimenting in independent study. It should be noted that highly capable teachers can maintain interest and enthusiasm in teaching primarily when they are working with highly capable students in small groups and individually or when they are lecturing to less able students in large groups where close contact is minimal. Likewise, highly capable students may maintain interest and enthusiasm for learning primarily when they are working with highly capable teachers as members of small groups and individually or, conceivably, when they are members of a large lecture section conducted by a less capable teacher with whom contact is minimal. Highly able teachers confronted constantly with a majority of less able students in small group or seminar sessions will produce very likely a situation detrimental to the teacher and to the student.

3. Elimination of constricting devices and elements such as required class attendance, required chapel attendance, the grade-point system, faculty involvement in student government, and student disciplinary matters.

4. Establishment of small housing units (34 students per unit) allowing closer contact, yet preserving privacy.

5. Introduction of a reading proficiency requirement which must be met ordinarily by the end of a student's freshman year.

6. Establishment of an open-stack library program in which the student has access to all works and periodicals in the library. Checking out books and periodicals is the responsibility solely of the student who is on his honor to uphold the library privileges extended to him. Nor is a library penalty charge made in the case of books retained beyond the specified return date.

7. Employment of an open-door classroom policy which per-

mits a student to sit in on any lecture of any instructor. (The same opportunity is also extended to every professor.) Under this definition of auditing and with permission of the instructor and faculty adviser a student may fulfill the requirements of any course, take a comprehensive examination, and be certified as having completed the course.

8. Initiation of the winter term (inter-semester) program in January of 1961. Credit for the winter term must be given to the curriculum planners for New College, Massachusetts; however, the definition of the term as a period of independent study is original with Florida Presbyterian College.

The winter term is a special four to five week period of independent study for all undergraduates. It comes between the fall semester, which begins early in September, and the spring semester, which begins early in February. With examinations for the fall semester over before the Christmas holidays, January is free for intensive study. Designed to develop the qualities of self-discipline in pursuits requiring the student to be the prime explorer, the winter term asks him to work without customary routine of classroom and lecture hall on a single problem growing out of his other studies or offered by a professor and to present his findings in final form. With guidance he elaborates and limits his subject, gathers material, organizes it, and presents it as a paper, a short story, a painting, a piece of laboratory equipment. During this special term each participating professor directs the activities of 12 to 15 students. The student may select a topic or a professor to work under. He may work with another student, a group, or by himself depending on the nature of the problem. Throughout the four weeks the professor is available for consultation and guidance and each student is expected to put in weekly 50 to 60 hours of study. This intensive, independent study supplements the extensive work of his courses and thus affords opportunity each of four years to engage in extended creative work not normally afforded in traditional undergraduate curriculums. In his freshman and sophomore years a student is encouraged to choose a topic outside of his major field of interest; in his junior and senior years he is encouraged to work in his major field. In the senior year this period may be devoted to research or study for the comprehensive examinations in the major field. Throughout the winter term at Florida Presbyterian College the student not only works on his own to master a limited subject but also he may have the benefit of step-by-step evaluation of his work. Annually, two-thirds of the faculty supervise projects. Others of the staff are free to do research and study of their own.

The procedure for executing the winter term is as follows. By October 1st certain professors submit one or two project proposals to the Academic Affairs Committee. This Committee accepts or rejects each proposal or asks that the proposal be redefined. By October 15th the prospectus of each offering is placed in the library for students to study. The student has until November 1st to rank in order of preference five of the many projects. These rankings are then forwarded to the registrar and he in turn places each student in one of the chosen programs. Actually most students are placed in one of the first three projects listed as most preferred. (This phase of the procedure assures a relatively equal balance in teaching load.) Students are then notified by November 10th of the project in which they will be engaged. At the same time professors are provided with a list of students with whom they will work and are encouraged to meet with their students prior to the Christmas vacation period for the purpose of laying the groundwork for the approaching study. Consequently, many students do preparatory work before and over the Christmas holidays. A special library orientation is conducted for freshman during the first few weeks of November.

This past year the study projects according to title were: Experimentation in Polymer Painting Medium, The *Essais* of Montaigne, The Theater of Jean Giraudoux, An Exercise in Ethnomusicology, Human Freedom, The Theology of Paul Tillich, Franz Kafka: Interpretation and Oral Readings, Evaluating Magazines, The Nature and Function of Symbols in Human Communication, The Works of Tennessee Williams, Imaginative Writing, Biblical Archaeology, A Study in American English Dialect, The Writings of Albert Camus, Great Personalities of the Christian Tradition, The Doctrine of Christian Vocation in Modern Perspective, Contemporary German Drama: Friedrich Durrenmatt in Particular, Experimental

Exploration of Social Factors in Fear, Explorations in Parapsychology, The Place of Troy in History, The Conquest of Mexico as Seen by Cortez and Diaz and the Aztecs, The Contemporary Scene in Mass Society, Ricardo's Theory of Economic Development, Conservatism in American Political Thought, Changing Values on the College Campus, Vector and Tensor Analysis, Set Theory, Analytic Inequalities, Studies in Animal Aggregations, Toxicological and Bio-chemical Studies of Several Animal Venoms and Toxins, Temperature Preferendum of Selected Aquatic Animals, Absorption of Nutrients from Sea Water by Invertebrates, Coherent and Incoherent Radiation, The Construction and Use of Models in Illustrating Chemical Phenomena, Synthesis and Stability of Polymer Latexes, Synthetic Muscle Machine, Mathematics in Western Culture, Color: Its Production and Perception, The Amplification of Physical Signals by Electronics, The Peaceful Uses of Atomic Energy.

Some of the projects are conducted in foreign countries. In 1962-1963 an interesting program carried 12 French-speaking students and their professor to Haiti. They lived in a student pension near the Institut Francais in Port-au-Prince. During the time spent in Haiti (December 23rd to January 29th) the students' mornings were devoted typically to discussions in French of selected works of contemporary Haitian literature. In the afternoon they read independently, concentrating on modern Haitian novels, for the purpose of writing in French a paper dealing with reflections of Haitian life in the novels as compared with their own observations. (Several of the novelists were available for consultation.) Each student who demonstrated unusual proficiency and interest in the language, and depending on the availability of research materials, was allowed to work on a topic of his own choice.

While the main purpose of this project was to strengthen the student's ability to speak, read, and write French, there were other factors which made this experience invaluable:

a. By living in a foreign country, rather than being merely a tourist, the student was required to develop his own initiative and adapt to a new environment.

b. By being forced to rely on French as his primary means

of communication, the student acquired a feeling for the language which no amount of classroom experience could provide.

c. By being placed among people whose religion, skin color, and mode of life are markedly different from his own, he had a rare opportunity to observe a foreign culture and to reflect upon his own prejudices and preconceived notions.

d. By being in a country which only a generation ago (1915-36) was subject to United States control, he had occasion to find out how "others see us."

e. Finally, as an intelligent, sympathetic visitor, he might contribute, albeit modestly, to understanding between peoples and nations.

In January of 1964 six professors and 72 students were involved in a winter-term study program in London. The specific projects in which they were engaged were The British Parliament and the Common Market Issue, The Treatment of Crime in Great Britain, The History of London, Art and Art Collections in England, British Music, and The Theatre in London. The students had specifically-assigned background materials on Great Britain to be read in advance of the trip; had assigned materials in connection with each project; had scheduled for them field experiences, lectures, and discussions to supplement library research at the University of London; and later prepared individual presentations of a creative-research nature.

In January of 1965 groups and professors will study in Greece, Jordan, and Spain. Full cost to the student for air transportation, room, board, guest lectures, books, and incidentals for the trip to Haiti was $230, to England $450, and projected as $600 for the forthcoming trip in 1965.

9. Provisions, under the heading of independent study, for students to take any course or program (listed or unlisted in the college catalog), to make up course deficiencies by comprehensive examination, and to pursue summer study at home according to each one's capabilities and secure the full recognition for work done which course credit normally certifies. Students engaged in such efforts must receive authorization from the respective instructor under whom the work is to be accomplished. The instructor defines all requirements and designates

a time at which the work will be submitted for evaluation and the examination taken. At the time the instructor notifies the registrar of his and the student's decision the student is duly entered into the course and his failure to complete the program as agreed to culminates in a grade of "U" (unsatisfactory).

10. Permission granted a student, with the endorsement of his major professor, to pursue thesis work in his junior and senior years. Normally certification equivalent to two-to-four courses and one winter term is awarded upon successful completion and defense of the thesis.

11. Initiating a core program which provides a common experience for all students, focuses sharply on group discussion and student leadership of group discussions in the advanced years. This program is a four-year plan of study drawing its staff from the faculty in all academic areas so that in any one year 60 per cent of the total faculty is involved. It is designed to provide the common educational experience for students regardless of field of specialization. Its subject matter is drawn from history, literature, economics, music, philosophy, religion, sociology, psychology, natural sciences—from the whole range of human inquiry and creativity. Underlying the design of the core program is the conviction that knowledge is unified and that at the heart of the academic experience there should be a unified, rather than departmentalized, approach to understanding.

The manner in which the subject matter of the program is selected, organized, and presented is determined by the objective of the course—"to equip the student for the formation and articulation of informed, independent, responsible judgments of value." The acquiring of specific information and the development of skill in analysis, dialectic, and writing receive attention as necessary preparation for value judgments.

The four semesters of the freshman and sophomore years are concerned with an examination of Western Civilization and Its Christian Heritage. The first semester's materials are drawn from the works and institutions of the contemporary world. The three following semesters treat the Hebrew and Greek sources of our culture, major issues of Medieval and Renaissance Europe, and then return to work and institutions of the modern world.

During these first two years students are assigned to small discussion groups which meet twice a week for an hour and a half each time. A member of the faculty leads each of these discussion groups, but they are not "classes" in the traditional sense of the term. The purpose of these sessions is to have the students examine, analyze, and discuss basic documents of our cultural and religious heritage. Papers are submitted regularly to discussion leaders for criticism and suggestions. Three hours a week are devoted to lectures, movies, plays during which the entire class meets together. A comprehensive examination at the end of the second year is the most important aspect of evaluation of the student's work in this program. Too, in the second semester of the sophomore year students are chosen to lead the weekly discussion sessions.

The third year course, Asian Studies, focuses the attention of the students on cultural forms, institutions, and historical movements which lie outside their own tradition and which are becoming increasingly significant for our civilization. One professor, a specialist in this area, has the primary instructional responsibility but many other members of the staff are called upon to present lectures on matters in which they have particular competence. There are two lectures and one small-group discussion session each week. Since the first two years of the core program have laid a foundation for initiative on the part of the students, considerable freedom is given to a student to follow lines of special interest in his reading and research, preferably in his major field. Student leaders are rotated in all discussion groups following briefing by the director of the program. Incidentally, this program is supported by annual conferences on Asia, elaborated biographical materials, language offerings in Chinese, cultural programs, and faculty institutes.

In the fourth year course, Christian Faith and Great Issues, persons of national and international reputation in economic, political, and scientific life are brought to the campus for lectures and informal discussions with the senior class. (Members of the entire college community are welcome to attend these lectures.) Preparatory lectures by members of the college faculty are coordinated on alternate weeks with the program of the visiting dignitaries. At the end of the fall and spring semesters students submit a personal journal on the issues considered during the semester and prepare an analysis of two periodicals in which they followed the issues during the course. It should be understood that this course was not designed to indoctrinate but to challenge students to think through some major social, economic, and political issues in the light of their own personal value systems—their own basic beliefs whatever they may be.

One of the assets which has been realized by the college as a result of its newness is this opportunity to build a core program around which departmental programs of specialization may be constructed.

12. Expectation that each freshman, near the close of the academic year, will prepare a tentative course program for the remaining three years of college and present it to his adviser for critical evaluation and counsel. At the end of the sophomore year he must submit for approval to the Committee on Academic Review his projected program as modified. At any time thereafter he may revise it with approval of his major professor. In this procedure each student is called upon to defend and to provide a rationale for his choice of courses. Vocational testing and counseling are available upon request or referral.

13. Introduction in 1963 of a student instructor program in which the most highly capable juniors and seniors are employed to assist professors in their teaching and research activities. These students are assigned office space and have office hours. Their duties range from tutoring fellow students and correcting papers to preparing bibliographies and checking references. At present there are 31 student instructors and projections indicate the employment of 75 such persons by 1968 at a salary of $400-500 per year per student instructor.

Each ensuing year other programs will be introduced thereby moving the faculty and students to a deeper immersion and development in independent study. In the spring of next year (1965) a course for all majors in certain disciplines will be taught in a modified independent study approach. Each instructor will meet his class once a week in an "X period" (a question and answer period with both the faculty member and student asking questions of each other) and students will meet at a scheduled period by themselves for formal discussion. A student leader is to be appointed for each discussion session. The professor should provide a syllabus for the course at the very onset and schedule regular tests if desired. There will be no formal lecture program.

In the summer of 1966 it is very likely that a 10-week summer session devoted entirely to research or independent study in the major field will be initiated. This will be recommended to students between their junior and senior years, depending upon the level of progress of the student. This may become a requirement for students contemplating graduate study. It is anticipated that this program will be patterned after the winter term period. By 1967 an independent study laboratory will be established and a revision of the structure of the major course programs will be under way.

Experience and evidence to date justify further exploration of independent study (though it is readily recognized that more sophisticated procedures of evaluation must be employed):

a. During the past three years ratings from systematic surveys of the students and faculty have revealed greatest preference for and enrichment derived from the winter term program of independent study. (The core and major course programs have followed closely each year.)

b. As students progress from the freshman to the senior year less supervision of their work is required during the winter term, without apparent loss in quality of work.

c. During the winter term the average student devotes 58 hours per week to active study on his project. Too, the rate of student failures is less in this period than in the preceding or succeeding semesters.

d. Over the past three years library circulation has shown greater increase in proportion to student body growth. Library circulation quadruples during the winter term program.

e. Over the past three years a greater proportion of the students has successfully completed work in independent study programs during the academic year (0%, 3%, 11%) and the respective summers (2%, 5%, 9%).

f. On the Nelson-Denny Reading Tests the average performance of the freshmen who had completed preparation for meeting the reading proficiency requirement was 749 words per minute with 87 per cent comprehension.

g. Performance of the two sophomore classes to date on the General Culture Test placed the average student at the 92nd percentile when compared with national norms.

h. Senior class mean percentiles on the Verbal, Quantitative and Advanced scales of the Graduate Record Examination were respectively 79th percentile, 75th percentile, and 69th percentile.

The Future

Nobody can say what the future holds for the program at Florida Presbyterian College, but we can now venture a guess. It is likely by 1984 that it will consist of a core course defined not as semester hours but as a lecture program that is open at all levels to all students, passed by a comprehensive examination, conducted still as mass lecture with discussion sessions for some students. Paralleling this core experience will be a major program which, like the core program, will be a lecture-discussion-laboratory program defined by all members within the discipline or department. Here, too, a comprehensive examination will be the final measure of competence. A comprehensive examination will also be employed for both areas of the curriculum (two of the following three: humanities, social sciences, natural sciences) outside of any student's major area. However, in this program the faculty in science working with the faculty in humanities will determine what is to be expected of a science major as to his knowledge of the humanities and likewise his knowledge of the social sciences. (I hope it can be clearly seen that the factor of interrelatedness of knowledge is equally vital.) By this time three-quarters of the faculty will be involved annually in the core program. This is referred to as a vertical approach to interdisciplinary study.

Another kind of impact comes through the comprehensive examinations worked out between divisions. This is referred to as the horizontal approach. Consequently, satisfactory performance in the comprehensive examinations indicated and possibly two foreign languages will be the requirements set by the college for graduation. There will be no semester program but a year-round program and few courses will be structured in the fashion in which they are now defined. There will be a point of matriculation and a point at which a degree is granted. Always level of accomplishment will be the prime determinant from beginning to end.

Such a program relies heavily on proficiency in reading, a student's ability to do independent study, the faculty member's interest in extending himself beyond his own particular academic discipline, and conceivably a new kind of devotion and respect for learning on the part of both student and teacher. Too, an atmosphere for independent study is a community attitude before it is the "way of life" of an institution and developing such a college attitude is determined by intellectual and financial resources. These factors and future experience will determine what Florida Presbyterian College will be in 1984.

Chapter 8

THE UNIVERSITY OF MICHIGAN DEARBORN CAMPUS

By W. E. STIRTON*

For the purpose of this volume it might well be that a description of the needs which the Dearborn Campus of the University of Michigan was designed to meet could well be rivaled in interest and importance by a recital of the unplanned and unexpected values which have resulted from the early operation of the Dearborn Campus. This narrative will therefore attempt to make a total presentation, or in the language of current automotive literature, a recital of "total performance."

The development of the Dearborn Campus of the University of Michigan, actually its genesis, lies in a statement by industry of their projection of need for quality manpower and of the University's response to that statement. A resulting and consequential gift of over $10,000,000 of private funds to the University allowed us to establish the Dearborn Campus with which this chapter is concerned.

It is a happy circumstance that this generous gift from industry to the University, predicated on the solution of a critical manpower problem, should develop an educational program which prepared "for the good living *and* the good life" and which additionally, we feel, makes a significant contribution to the strengthening of the local community educational assets and a pertinent pointer for the direction of other state-wide programs. Perhaps the very fact that these multiple objectives are being proven completely compatible is merely a confirmation and reaffirmation of the fundamental truth that American

---

*Mr. Stirton is Vice President and Director of the Dearborn Center, University of Michigan, Dearborn, Michigan.

education must simultaneously achieve many goals in order to meet its total obligation to the individual and to society. Or better still, perhaps we will more promptly come to the realization that we can no longer afford the luxury of the "either-or" concept. I refer to the vicious notion which has plagued us so long that it must be *either* education for professional competency *or* for the cultural attributes and that appreciation for professional and occupational competency cannot be reconciled with a "culture" curriculum.

Actually, an educational analysis of the Dearborn Campus begins simultaneously with an appraisal of the first sentence descriptive of the origin of the Campus. It is of primary significance that *industry came to education* for the development of this Campus.

All of us who have spent any time in education have pleaded for cooperation between industry and education and we have talked piously of the "two-way street" leading to that cooperation. It is, however, unfortunately true that while the street may permit two directional traffic, most of the traffic is only one way, from education to industry with relatively little reciprocal traffic. And in altogether too many instances the trips to industry have been made by educators with a tin cup in their hands and a proposal in their hip pockets.

For years higher education and industry have wistfully talked about cooperative planning but seldom, if ever, has there been a demonstration of such cooperation in planning as that which resulted in the establishment of the recently opened Dearborn Campus of the University of Michigan, located appropriately enough in the heart of industrial Michigan, in the center of its greatest concentration of population. Paradoxically, the hub of this industrial concentration is the hundreds of wooded acres surrounding the Fair Lane residence of the late Henry Ford. Located at this hub are completed buildings comprising the Dearborn Campus of a great university serving as a functioning and living monument to cooperative planning.

In our case when industry came to education, and I again emphasize the direction of travel, they came with a basic quality manpower need. They brought with them manpower tables which, as in the case with most industrial manpower analyses, were projected for the years ahead with surprising accuracy and care. These tables of specific manpower needs indicated three basic shortage of deficiency areas:

1. Numbers of available "quality" professional personnel.
2. The requirement of keeping instruction "current" in light of the rapidly evolving technological changes particularly characteristic of their area.
3. The excessive "turnover" or low retention of such personnel.

After the problem presentation by industry there followed many meetings, some on campus, some in the industrial setting. There were reports from special curriculum groups and studies of new educational installations in other areas. From these and other forms of stimulating interchange emerged the recommendation that the University undertake its first full fledged venture into a program of truly cooperative education, in physical facilities on a new campus located in the heart of the industrial complex of southeastern Michigan.

In essence this arrangement would meet the trio of shortages described by industry since:

1. New physical facilities appropriately located would accommodate the needed additional numbers.
2. A truly "cooperative" educational program could provide the intimate, intensive, and immediate relationship with the technological developments essential for "current" instruction.
3. The mutual acquaintance and subsequent understanding, appreciation, and respect between "co-oping" student and employer would predict and nearly guarantee longevity of employment.

Later in this chapter I shall expand on these three basic and generating elements.

In spite of the early prominence we have given to a recital of values to industry in the program it would, of course, not constitute justification for program implementation if there had not been earlier clear and convincing evidence of basic values for students. In a recitation of "values" for students I am of course recounting the values over and above the common and accepted values of education per se. Certainly these "over and above" values for the students in the program would include the following:

1. Occupational guidance or sound and early vocational choice from direct industrial contact.
2. Enriched instruction with demonstrable application of theory to practice.
3. Additional motivation and development of mature judgment.
4. Understanding of the world of work and "how to get along with people."
5. Significant remuneration.

An elaboration of the values to participating employers of the cooperative program would include:

1. Opportunity for comprehensive and thorough evaluation before employment thus greatly reducing "turn-over" (this is equally of value for students with respect to potential employers).
2. "Currency" of instruction with direct relationship to employer needs.
3. Realistic management to labor orientation.
4. Automatic recruitment intake and a continual flow of potential employees passing under supervisory appraisal and evaluation on challenging and determining work assignments without any implication of employment precommitment.
5. Exploratory induction and orientation opportunities.
6. Out-of-state and overseas plant procedure orientation for appropriate students.

This somewhat cursory recital of values both to the student and to the employer might so far seem rather prosaic and routine. Such superficial judgments have long plagued occupationally oriented educational undertakings. In our case this is aggravated by a lack of agreement on basic definitions. Educators have long been known for their disposition and facility for conjuring up words and phrases to describe educational innovations, undertakings, and indeed sometimes to disguise older concepts with new verbal wrappings. Carried to its undesirable and confusing extreme it is sometimes used to simulate erudition. Certainly there has been much confusion as a result of the "flexibility" of the educator's vocabulary. There are many who fail to distinguish among flexibility, fluency, clarity, and just ordinary verbosity. Specifically it is hard indeed to get any kind of agreement on the understanding of words in the professional educational programs such as "single-skill," "vocational," "occupational," "technical," "sub-professional," "professional," *ad infinitum* and nearly *ad nauseam*. This same multiplicity of interpretations and shadings applies to "cooperative" programs. This poses a problem of interpretation for the Dearborn Campus too. Specifically we refer to the definition of our cooperative program in definitely different terms from those which are used sometimes to describe what is actually a planned interruption of school attendance with a temporary job, coupled sometimes so that two students will share these joint interruptions or intermittent school attendance and job placement.

In the case of the Dearborn Campus we would be entirely remiss if we did not take full advantage of the unusual assets which allow us to construct a cooperative program of unique educational significance. These assets include as a paramount value the environment of the campus in the heart of the industrial area of southeastern Michigan. We also capitalize on the great asset revealed in the first statement regarding the establishment of the Dearborn Campus, namely that "industry came to education." Under these circumstances and stimulations education can be highly directive and selective in determining the work assignments of the students. It is imperative in our judgment that these work assignments be highly correlated with the instructional program. This means, for example, that if a young man in an engineering cooperative program is to spend a portion of his work assignment on a dynamometer then it is important for our coordinator, working with the industrial supervisor, to know the nature of the test operations on that dynamometer. Then we can properly determine what competencies the young man must have when going on that dynamometer assignment in the way of preparation in mechanics, thermodynamics, physics, calculus, and so on. It is equally important that we know how long it will require to absorb the instructional values that are pertinent and that result from this assignment on the dynamometer. At the expiration of that determined time the student must then move onward and upward in work assignments, in phase with his instructional program and at a rate compatible with his educational growth. Under these guidelines the work assignment is truly a related and pertinent part of the educational program. The employer is truly a partner in the educational venture and should be so regarded. The student is really not an employee of the company but is truly serving an industrial or business internship. Indeed, in our state of Michigan, in harmony with this concept we were fortunate in having the state legislature re-define cooperative education so that students while on the work assignments or internships are not eligible for unemployment insurance, since they are continually to be identified as students of the University and not employees of the company. Indeed, in the Dearborn Campus arrangement we require that our students pay a fee while they are on their work assignment. This student fee, while less than the on-campus fee, provides for those "off-campus" students while on their work assignments such needs as the industrial coordinator service, library facilities, evaluation of industrial reports, and identical access and admissibility to athletic and social privileges of the University whether they are on the "industrial campus" or on the "college campus." It is difficult indeed to appraise all the values that accrue, not only to the student and to the University but also to the employer, when the employer is considered truly a partner in the educational venture. Parenthetically, we have these "partners" meet regularly on our Campus with both our coordinators and our faculty for the purpose of mutual communication and joint planning.

Certainly without this partnership concept with employers and the internship concept with students it would not be possible to achieve the currency and the vitality of instruction that is a hallmark of the true cooperative program, the basis on which we may properly use the word "internship," not "job." This value of vitality of instruction is obviously one of the most desired attributes of the new educational program that must evolve to meet the rapidly changing educational requirements of our increasingly automated and industrialized society. A not insignificant value of such relationship is the resulting intimacy of association and improvement of understanding that applies between industry and education. Obviously this improvement not only serves industry well in terms of more readily available information and assistance in their industrial problems; it also serves the University well in terms of industrial support for appropriation requests and legislative understandings and total appreciation.

Earlier in this chapter reference was made to the fortuitous combination of circumstances that permitted the University to plan a program to meet industrial needs while at the same time it developed a pattern for a possible solution of pending educational problems. In the state of Michigan we have a most unfortunate disparity in the proportion of young people attending church related and other private institutions beyond high school, compared to those in attendance at tax-aided and tax-supported institutions. The present percentage indicates about 18 per cent in the private schools and 82 per cent in various types of tax-supported institutions. In spite of a very real and very general dedication to the dual system of education, the economic pattern of society predicts rather clearly that there will be relatively small expansion of private institutions in the future. The bulk of educational facility expansion to meet the increased enrollments of the future must be a responsibility of the tax-aided institutions and that expansion in Michigan will be particularly aggravated and severe because of the paucity of private and church-related institutions.

Therefore, the role of the community college is even more important in Michigan than it is in many other states. There is general agreement that the role of the community college must include the following primary elements:

1. To provide the terminal, occupational, or technical vocational programs required for competencies in those fields requiring perhaps two years beyond high school but not necessarily demanding a degree.

2. To provide wide and generous opportunities for the establishment and conduct of adult education programs in the areas necessary in the community.

3. To provide college parallel programs for appropriate youth of the community, particularly those who cannot afford the luxury of living away from home while attending school or those who for other reasons desire to be close to their point of residence.

Accepting these three primary roles of the community college and with recognition of the fact that in the Dearborn community there already existed a splendid community college (Henry Ford Community College), the University determined to use its resources and the support of the founding gift in the establishment of programs beginning at the junior year. Therefore, the Dearborn Campus is and always has been a collection of senior colleges or divisions. There are no freshmen or sophomores; only juniors, seniors, and graduate students are enrolled. This means that the Dearborn Campus then is entirely a "transfer" campus and subject to many vicissitudes of that restrictive pattern.

It is difficult to communicate the special purpose of the Dearborn Campus to prospective students with only "delayed access" to high school graduates without it being interpreted as recruiting away from established four year colleges. We also have a very basic difficulty of general interpretation in that the Dearborn Campus *is* the University of Michigan and operates under exactly the same requirements for admission of students at the junior, senior, and graduate levels. This means that many students in "college parallel" programs in other institutions might not be accepted on the Dearborn Campus and it means also that students in other programs of the community colleges have even greater difficulty in being accepted.

On the other hand this basic philosophical concept of the University, of not interferring with but rather enhancing and supporting and strengthening the program of the community college, has some real values. For example, in the state of Michigan, as is the case of every other state, we have many small communities which are dependent for economic and indeed physical survival in large measure upon relatively few local industries. These local industries in turn find real difficulty in attracting and retaining quality manpower because of difficulties in convincing inexperienced youth unacquainted with their plant of their present attractiveness and their potential for growth.

We have found that we can offer very real service to such communities which acutely require the retention of their youth in order that they may retain their future. We have repeatedly held meetings in such communities with the officials of the nearby community college and the employer groups. We make arrangements for early identification of appropriate students in the community college who later enroll on the Dearborn Campus and alternate their attendance on our campus with appropriately selected internships in the industry of their local community. Upon graduation from the University of Michigan through its Dearborn Campus these young people have earned and received the same degree they would have received from the main campus of the University and at the same time they have been through the internship of work assignments with their local community industry. Since these young people's roots are in that community, as witness the fact that they graduated from the local community college, and since they have had opportunity to become acquainted with and impressed by the local industry and the local industry in turn has become impressed by their competencies through the work assignment, the probability is that this employment will be one of a long lasting nature. Thus the community college, the youth of the community, and the employer in the community have been well served by the Dearborn Campus of the University of Michigan.

An interesting extension of this concept is its application to a large employer with subsidiary plants in various states. In such circumstance the youth of State X might come to the Dearborn Campus and arrange that the alternate assignments which take him into the industrial internship be so selected that the young person has a wide industrial orientation in the parent plant. This means that when such a student returns to his native state and to the subsidiary plant in that state, he returns with a degree from the University and with a thorough orientation, indoctrination, and knowledge of the procedures in the parent plant which make him unusually valuable to the subsidiary plant. Note that since first enrollment on the Dearborn Campus is at the junior level, the student might well come as a transfer, as a State X community college graduate, or as a transfer from another college in State X. This type of arrangement is most rewarding when the local originating college and the plant in State X have jointly participated in the planning with the parent plant in our area and the Dearborn Campus. When a student graduates from the Dearborn Campus and has completed his selectively planned internship in the parent plant, his return to his home community and employment in the branch plant in his home community reflects creditably on the originating school and the local community as well as the plants involved and the Dearborn Campus.

An interesting further expansion of this concept is in its application to overseas plants and subsidiaries of basic American corporations. Under such circumstances we enroll on the Dearborn Campus students from the foreign lands where these subsidiary plants are located. Their "internships" then are directed through careful planning with the parent plant in this country. At the conclusion of their internship experiences and the academic requirements of the Dearborn Campus they return to their native country. They take back with them much more than a degree from the University of Michigan. They have profited from a carefully planned internship far more intensive and extensive than the "orientation" exposure commonly provided new employees. Additionally we hope they have acquired, by continual association, an exposure to the free enterprise system which should serve in good stead against pressures of other ideologies in their native land. And of importance to the employer, he is being assisted to meet the common requirement of these overseas countries to employ a high and often stipulated percentage of nationals in such overseas plants.

We should be remiss if we did not acknowledge that other educational institutions have for years had comparable programs in many fields where we are now only initiating such patterns. It is true that the application of the "internship" concept on the work assignment is more difficult to achieve within the liberal arts. Such arrangements are rather special and must be custom tailored to fit the circumstance. We hope additionally to develop cooperative programs with this same "internship" concept in the education of graduates as industrial biologists and chemists and in areas such as state and trade association secretaries. It might be mentioned too that the program of teacher certification, both at the elementary and the secondary levels on the Dearborn Campus as well as in other installations, is a program very closely related to the true cooperative program. The one outstanding difference is that the students in such programs very seldom receive any significant remuneration. It should be mentioned, parenthetically, that the students on the Dearborn Campus in the cooperative program have average earnings over $1850 per term exclusive of the fringe benefits of seniority, stock option purchase, pension rights, and the like which they are awarded if they accept employment at graduation with the employer to whom they had been assigned on their "co-op" program. Indeed the general pattern is that the employer credits the "co-op" student upon his graduation with plant service and employment credit equal to the time he was enrolled in the cooperative program. In such values these students are therefore about three years ahead of graduates of traditional programs.

This chapter may have seemed to place undue emphasis throughout on the cooperative aspects of the program on the Dearborn Campus. If this be the case it is not intentional and merely reflects the fact that the literature, science, and the arts program represent a long established and irrevocable commitment of the University of Michigan undertaking while the cooperative program is a relatively new experience to the University. But all through the planning period when the specifications were being worked out with industry to determine the magnitude of their gift to establish the Dearborn Campus, there was the strong emphasis on the liberal arts component of both the engineering and business administration programs that characterizes a total educational program of any great university. The liberal arts program has always been an integral component of the Dearborn Campus program, has been of service to the engineering and business administration "co-op" programs, and has been a degree granting program in its own right. Its major undertaking as a Liberal Arts Division is in response to overwhelming community need for the state certification of elementary and secondary teachers, certification which graduates receive concurrently with their liberal arts degrees from the University.

All the previous discussion and description properly prefaces a statement of basic dedication of the Dearborn Campus. It is our strong conviction that this nation can no longer afford the luxury of division which now attends educational institutions and purposes. Those who commit and perpetuate this separation say in essence that one pattern may train professionals but the other educates people. They make an "either-or" distinction that cannot fit appropriately into the current American scene and requirements. There is no reason whatever logically to assume that the educating of young people to earn a good living in established and needed professional undertakings such as engineering or business administration must or does in any way deprive them of the ability to lead a good life with appreciation of all of those values and disciplines that make it so.

This chapter is not written by a psychologist nor by a sociologist nor has it been reviewed by such persons; consequently the comments which follow are made without benefit of clergy. Every one who has worked in technical or vocational education at the secondary or the college level is aware of the indictment of such education as a "second class" educational citizen. This indictment is manifest in various ways but in any of its manifestations, real or fancied, implied or inferred, it is to a very real and significant degree a completely negative and thoroughly undesirable element. Conversely we know that the labeled "opponents" of technical or professional programs are too often considered impractical, non-realistic, ivory-towered academicians. Such identification is equally negative and reprehensible.

Students become involved in this divisiveness. Fallacious prestige concepts are developed which pre-determine occupational selection and introduce and engender other undesirable elements in educational endeavor.

There is evidence indeed of this same division in industry. What does the potential employer desire of the educational system? Does he want the well-rounded, the generalist, or the specifically and singly trained? There is even common discussion that such a choice varies with the industrial echelon, the aloof and removed president, or the employment supervisor "on the firing line."

Without extending the debate which is probably more accurately identified as a "filibuster," it is our opinion that we can no longer afford the luxury of making a choice where no choice should or need be made and then trusting that in subsequent years the error of making that choice can and will be rectified. Perhaps other more competent authors in other more appropriate texts will analyze and resolve the reason the "either-or" syndrome exists. Perhaps there is some simple, easy way to make it disappear.

In the meantime we are attempting to destroy the "either-or" element by demonstration. We hope that every faculty man in every field is satisfied that we not only need not but must not choose nor suffer the student or employer to choose. The power of example, the persuasiveness of dedicated teaching, and most conclusively the performance and productivity and participation of our graduates will be the ultimate demonstration of how well we have served in our endeavor.

In this connection it is pertinent to note that the most generous gift of industry to the University which established the Dearborn Campus also included the Fair Lane estate of the late Henry and Clara Ford. The Dearborn Campus is close enough (35 minutes drive) to provide convenient access to the cultural and athletic events and other facilities of the Ann Arbor campus. It is only 15 minutes from downtown Detroit.

Though in the very heart of one of the world's great industrial areas the Dearborn Campus is hidden away in a forest. It is a wooded wonderland which once was picked by the richest man in the world as his private paradise, stocked with song birds brought over from England, enhanced with streams, ponds, nature trails, and formal gardens. The land is an ancient link between Detroit and the Ann Arbor campus. A century ago it was the sight of the famous Ten Eyk Tavern, a way station on the Ann Arbor Trail.

Then the world changed—due in no small part to the efforts of a man who had been born in the neighborhood and had formed his guiding ideas here, a man who, while transforming the surrounding countryside into a vast industrial complex, sought to retain in this particular haven the beauty and serenity of a by-gone era. Here in his limestone castle on a grassy bank of the River Rouge, Henry Ford lived for a third of a century making history and challenging it, erupting in ideas which sometimes thrilled and sometimes dismayed the worldwide public to whom his every word was news and ruling with regal sway over an individual industrial empire the like of which the world had never seen before and perhaps may never see again.

Alongside the famous rose gardens has risen a sleek cluster of laboratories, classrooms, and other installations that are as fine and modern as money can buy. The fabled mansion now serves as a scene of conferences and seminars of national and international scope. The beauty and quiet seclusion of the campus provides an exceptional environment for learning.

In our total environment—physical, industrial, and philosophical—we feel that we have a rich laboratory for demonstrating that we need not and must not in American education make a choice between provision for a good living and provision for a good life. We on the Dearborn Campus feel that we have the opportunity to demonstrate that the American way is to accept both as the total responsibility of the American educational pattern.

Chapter 9

EDUCATIONAL INNOVATION AT MICHIGAN STATE UNIVERSITY

By PAUL L. DRESSEL*

In the fall of 1942 Michigan State University enrolled 6,467 students; in this past fall, 1963, the on-campus enrollment was 27,669. This growth in enrollment has taken place despite marked increase in admissions standards. Unless there are further and marked increases in the standards of admission or a significant expansion of higher education facilities in the state of Michigan, the on-campus enrollment will reach (by 1972) anywhere from 42,000 to 52,000 students. An enrollment of this magnitude is certainly not desired, but it may be unavoidable. In such a rapidly growing university, innovation has been necessarily the order of the day.

The word "innovation" has been chosen with care. Although we at Michigan State, like other institutions of higher education, often speak loosely of "experimentation," there is little that can be truly called experimentation in higher education. Despite the existence at Michigan State since 1944 of an Office of Evaluation Services, charged with evaluation of curriculum and instructional developments, and the more recently established Office of Institutional Research, evaluation has been largely directed to the understanding and the improvement of innovations rather than to the comparison of experimental programs with standard or traditional ones. Even innovation must be considered a relative term, for programs new in a particular institution are not necessarily original. Too frequently one innovation follows so rapidly upon another that evaluation becomes an exercise in futility. An evaluation of an already modi-

*Mr. Dressel is Director of the Office of Institutional Research, Michigan State University, East Lansing, Michigan.

fied or discarded program is seldom accepted as significant in planning for change. However, it is certainly true that the rapid growth of Michigan State and the consequent inevitable changes in its character have developed a dynamic atmosphere in which interesting new ideas have usually achieved quick support from administration and faculty alike.

Michigan State University shares with almost every other college and university the view that its very founding was an innovation of primary importance. With the usual slight exaggeration, Michigan State lays claim to having started in 1855 as the pioneer land-grant college, and various statements have attested to a large number of "firsts," all of which would no doubt be hotly disputed by other institutions elsewhere in these United States. However, we are not here concerned with the distant past, nor are we concerned with claiming firsts. We are talking primarily of innovations of recent vintage, for any innovation which exists unchanged for as much as ten years may have become a tradition which hinders rather than helps the adjustment of the institution to changing conditions. However, there are a few "traditional" educational innovations which require comment because they are still in existence and are perhaps even more viable than when they were initiated.

Twenty years ago the Basic College was founded to provide to all undergraduates a minimal common general education experience. Although many changes have been made, including changing the name from Basic College to University College, the essential objectives of the program remain the same. As a second long-time innovation we may note that, for well over thirty years, the University has permitted students to acquire credit by examination in any course offered in the University. The provision was seldom used until the Basic College came into existence. From that time on, credit by examination became an accepted fact of life which was further underscored by the advent of veterans and a little later of the Honors College. Although many of our faculty members have expressed amazement both at the national attention given this development in recent years and at the furor occasionally created on other campuses by attempts to inaugurate such a policy, honesty compels the admission that, aside from the University College courses, a student who would acquire credit by examination must have a high degree of persistence as well as the necessary competencies. Clearly one man's innovation is another's irritation.

RECENT INNOVATION

But enough of history. We are concerned with recent activity and with plans for the future. Spurred on by a rapidly growing student body (especially at the graduate level) in a period in which financial stringencies have not permitted corresponding expansion in the faculty, all of the colleges and departments of the University have found it necessary to re-examine their activities. Not unnaturally, much of this attention has been focused on the curriculum and the instructional program where the increased burden has been most apparent.

University College

The University College especially has been beset by numbers, and so efforts have been devoted to finding new ways to carry on instruction with no diminution of quality. For example, in the Department of American Thought and Language, lay readers, principally faculty wives and other women in the community with backgrounds in English or other relevant disciplines, have been used to assist departmental faculty in the reading of student papers. There is some evidence that the paper reading is done as well or even more conscientiously by these readers than by full-time faculty and that the results are as good if not better than before. It even appears that some of the faculty are pleased to be relieved of this chore! In the Department of Natural Science nearly half of the course has been developed in programed materials which have been found to be extremely effective in promoting student learning and in providing a degree of individualization in learning which would otherwise not be possible with present enrollments.

Not all of the attention, however, has focused on means of accommodating large numbers of students. The Department of Social Science, recognizing the extreme involvement of the University in international education programs and the relatively small extent to which this involvement had affected undergraduates, undertook to emphasize international affairs by reorganizing the courses. For this purpose the faculty has written and edited eleven books published in paperback form. Both the Humanities Department and the Department of American Thought and Language have placed increased emphasis on informal extraclass activities for students involving films, drama, or other carefully planned programs. The University College also responded to the demand of students for a senior seminar by organizing a course in "Great Issues," an elective course for seniors. The staff for this course has been sought from the total University.

The Office of Evaluation Services, a unit in the University College assigned responsibilities for examination development and for general evaluation activity, took note of the fact that many apparently well-prepared students were enrolling in University College courses rather than risking the possibility of not passing the examinations which were scheduled at the close of the quarter. Accordingly, the Evaluation Services staff, with the assistance of the instructional departments, developed a set of short waiver examinations offered at the beginning of each quarter. The student acquiring the waiver privilege may either take other work to make up the credits or may, if he wishes, take the regular examination at the end of the next quarter at which it is offered and attempt to gain full credit by meeting the standards on that examination.

When the University College was organized the possibility was introduced that students might enroll without indicating a major. In the course of time these no-preference students, as they are called, became the direct advising responsibility of the University College. At present more than 3,000 students are in this no-preference category, and the University College has, of necessity, expended much energy in planning and carrying through an effective advisory program.

Other Colleges

Other colleges of the University have also been actively involved in educational innovation. A few examples must suffice to suggest the nature of this activity. The College of Engineering has recently undertaken to revise the undergraduate program, placing far more emphasis on basic mathematics and science and reducing much of the undergraduate engineering specialization. The College of Business has been reorganizing its program, placing more emphasis on mathematics and statistics and on the basic social sciences. The College of Home Economics has put greater emphasis on liberal education elements in its program and considerably reduced the common core required of the several home economics majors. The College of Veterinary Medicine has developed a year-round program accompanied by condensation of courses into larger credit blocks. Each course will be offered twice during the year, thereby increasing both the efficiency in the use of facilities and the number of students that can be handled in the program. The College of Education has been involved in extensive reorganization as well as in restudy of curriculum. In many ways, however, one of the more significant developments is that of reorganization of the teacher education programs to involve greater participation from the subject matter fields and to insure that instruction in these areas is more responsive to the many changes going on in elementary and secondary school curricula. A four-year elementary intern program, requiring summer session attendance at the end of the sophomore and junior years but culminating in a paid one-year internship in the senior year, has been developed.

Two or three years ago the conclusion was reached that the College of Arts and Sciences had become such a large enterprise that coordination was rendered difficult. Furthermore, it appeared that the varying problems of the different groups of disciplines made it difficult, if not impossible, either to think constructively about the improvement of the undergraduate program or to establish close working relationships with various professional schools. As a result this unit has been broken into three colleges: the College of Natural Science, the College of Social Science, and the College of Arts and Letters. Each of these colleges has undertaken to review its undergraduate program with the intention of developing a broader and better liberal arts program. Since most of these studies are still under way, it is not possible to report just what will finally emerge. Two examples, however, will indicate some of the thinking going on. The college is proposing a reduction in the maximum number of hours which a student would be permitted to take in any one department, thus increasing both the emphasis on a broad liberal education and on the electing of courses from departments and disciplines immediately related to the major. This pattern has been designated as a radial major. In the College of Natural Science a single introductory biological science course is being planned which will provide the initial experience for all majors in any one of the biological science departments.

Advising

The College of Education has established an Advisement Center, available to students at all hours of the day, which attempts to separate advisement from enrollment and registration. This area of advising has been one of increasing concern in the University, for the large numbers of students have forced an increase in the number of advisees per faculty member while the increasing class size and the increasing emphasis on graduate study have decreased the amount of time which the faculty members have available for conferring with students. All of the colleges at Michigan State have been concerned with this matter, and we are presently in the initial throes of thinking about a thorough-going study of the total advisory problem.[1] One possibility which must be given serious attention is that of separating broad educational advising and planning from detailed questions regarding particular courses or curriculums which can be answered only by the teaching faculty directly involved.

Residence Halls

Many of the more interesting current innovations are developed around our newer residence halls. These halls are co-educational in the sense that one wing is assigned to men, the

---

[1] It is my observation that advising is generally in a deplorable state in most institutions of higher education, small colleges as well as large universities. The difficulty seems to me to reside in the fact that very few faculty members have any real conception of what an undergraduate liberal education should be, and they seldom know much about courses and programs other than those in their own immediate area.

other to women, and the connecting intermediate area to class-rooms, offices, recreational, and dining facilities. There has been an attempt in all residence halls to reduce the competition in athletics, decorations, and the like and to replace these activities by art exhibits, musical recitals, and other cultural events. One interesting example is that of an international emphasis one evening a week. This is accomplished by planning a special meal which includes foods characteristic of a given country, inviting as guests foreign students who are natives of that country, and having available films from the Embassy for showing and discussion after dinner. Other interesting programs have been built around special discussion group projects, such as marital relations, women's role in the economy, and discussion of student leadership problems. The Case-Wilson-Wonders residence hall complex has been heavily used by lower division students, including many no-preference students. This group decided that it would be helpful to the residents to plan a *Majors Night* to which were invited representatives of all of the colleges and most of the departments of the University. This was found to be highly successful.

In each residence hall there is a head adviser who is usually an advanced doctoral candidate in student personnel work with a number of years of prior experience in residence halls. There are two graduate advisers who, if not in student personnel work, are taking graduate study in closely related fields, and there is one advanced undergraduate resident assistant per fifty students. There has been increasing emphasis on the organization of the residence halls into "houses" with considerable autonomy, each "house" being operated around a group of students assigned to a resident assistant. This has tended to break the large residence hall down into smaller and more closely knit groups of students.

Residence Hall-Based Instruction

About three years ago, when attention was being given to the planning of several new residence halls, there was discussion of the possibility of developing a number of experimental liberal arts colleges, each with a distinctive program which would provide a common educational experience to all students in a single residence hall. The thought was that each hall should be a quasi-independent unit having its own faculty. The students would have had much of their educational experience in the hall but would also have had available the instructional resources of the University in advanced fields. The reaction of the faculty to this proposal can only be described as violent. In retrospect it is difficult to say whether this negative reaction resulted primarily because the plan was revealed without having gone through the usual interminable discussions in various faculty committees or because it was regarded as a threat to the existing college and departmental structure. In any case it became necessary to take another approach.

The first three new halls—Case, Wilson, and Wonders—were assigned to the University College for the development of an in-hall academic program. Each of these three halls houses 1,200 students. They include a total of 14 classrooms, six laboratories, 47 offices, an auditorium, a kiva, a library, and five conference rooms. The total classroom seating space accommodates 1,750 students and the offices house 58 faculty members. In the fall of 1963, seven colleges and 16 departments were offering 101 sections of 19 different courses in these facilities. The classroom space has been used at a much higher level of efficiency than in other portions of the campus and, furthermore, the classrooms are open in the evening to provide students study areas. The kiva is also used for cultural programs. The Department of Music and the Department of Speech and Dramatics have arranged a number of events on a weekly basis in this hall complex and the students are each charged only $1.00 for fifteen different events. Registration for courses in the complex is restricted to students residing there and simplified procedures have been made available for them to pick up enrollment cards for courses offered in their residence area.

One of the reasons for introducing classroom activity into the residence halls has been the increasing size of the campus and the resulting time and effort required in getting from one place to another. Because of this space-time pressure students have generally been enrolled in two-hour blocks in classes in the residence hall. These classes operate on a slightly different schedule so that when the students complete a two-hour block in the residence hall and move back to the main campus for classes they will have a somewhat longer interval than the usual ten-minute interim.

Numerous evaluations of the Case-Wilson-Wonders educational program have been carried out. Some of these have been opinion surveys of faculty and students, others have looked at more objective data. Generally, it may be said that faculty and students alike enjoy the closer contact possible under these circumstances. Studies of student grades, making due allowance for ability, indicate that students housed in and taking work in a residence hall area have tended to do slightly better work than other students enrolled in the same course. The examination of such evidence convinces us that the residence hall instructional program: eliminates wasted time and energy, reduces the inconveniences involved in long treks from residence halls to classes, strengthens the quality of the living experience and of the academic experience by so interrelating them that each reinforces the other, provides an opportunity to study the implications and possibilities of some decentralization of student activities and student personnel functions, permits exploration of other patterns of faculty organization than the departmental structure as the basis for operation of undergraduate educational programs, alleviates the shortage of instructional space and improves the utilization of space by making recreational areas serve a dual purpose, develops in students an increased sense of responsibility for their own education, and brings faculty and students together on common grounds of shared concerns and interests.

For those of us who had been enthused about the possibility of developing a number of independent liberal arts colleges in the several residence halls, the program falls far short of our hopes, but the general enthusiasm and satisfaction which have been evidenced in the freshman and sophomore students oriented to the Case-Wilson-Wonders complex have provided the basis for planning similar developments in new residence halls for upper division students.

This past fall when McDonel Hall opened, it was made the headquarters of the Science and Mathematics Teaching Center which is a combined effort of the College of Education and the

College of Natural Science. The program here really did not get under way until the winter quarter, so it is not possible to say much about the details or anything about the success. However, the staff members assigned to the offices there are connected with the science departments or with the College of Education. The staff is interested in the interdepartmental courses in the sciences, especially in the development of the common introductory course in biological science mentioned earlier. The Center also provides a departmental home for students with interdepartmental science interests. The Center is also especially concerned with elementary education, particularly emphasizing the problems of teaching science at that level.

Two additional residence halls are under construction which will be put into use next fall. One of these has been assigned to the College of Social Science, the other to the College of Arts and Letters. Since students in any one of these three colleges (Natural Science-Social Science-Arts and Letters) are likely to be taking some courses from one of the other colleges, it seems possible to regard these three residence halls as forming another complex which may provide a fairly sizeable proportion of the course experience for the advanced students housed in the area. Again, however, the planning is in initial stages and it is not possible to be specific.

THE EDUCATIONAL DEVELOPMENT PROGRAM

Many of the innovations which have been described in preceding paragraphs could be subsumed under a broader program of innovations which has been labeled the Educational Development Program. This program embraces a number of purposes. One has already been described at some length in connection with the residence hall instruction program. The Educational Development Program also includes a complete review of curriculum offerings in an effort to reduce overlapping and duplication in courses and to combine small credit courses into larger blocks which will permit more efficient planning of instruction and more efficient utilization of both student and instructor time. The program is also concerned with the exploration of new developments in educational technology which may enhance the quality of learning and which may, at the same time, release some faculty time for curriculum planning, for research, and for other important activities. In this connection, the program embraces the idea of developing what has tentatively been called a Learning Resources Center which would supply both the human and electronic resources necessary for analyzing course and curricular purposes and developing the best possible instructional program to meet these goals. The Educational Development Program has also placed emphasis on assigning the student more responsibility for his own education and involves, therefore, attention to an increase in the amount of independent study activity and the use of examinations for advanced credit.

Within the framework of these broad goals work has been proceeding in the various colleges and departments. Small grants have been made available to departments interested in experimentation or in study of curricular or instructional revision. The use of film and video-tape, as well as programed instruction and various combinations of lecture and discussion groups, are representative of some of the developments currently under way. The progress of the Educational Development Program has been slowed by the inavailability of funds to provide adequate staffing for the very extensive study of curricula and courses as well as for the advisement of the faculty on the various technological resources available and their possible applicability to various instructional problems. With the coordination now being supplied by a director of the Educational Development Program (and by several full-time associates to be appointed shortly), many of the problems which require concentrated university-wide attention before thorough-going revision can be initiated at the college and departmental level will be attacked and, hopefully, resolved. Steady forward movement should soon become evident.

The Economics of Innovation

There has too long been the assumption that if one is concerned with quality, costs of education must not be critically examined. There is sufficient evidence readily available in every institution of higher education to make it clear that increased quality is by no means inconsistent with increased efficiency and economy. If the major goal of an undergraduate education is to prepare students to continue their education, then the tremendous proliferation of courses characteristic of our undergraduate programs is unnecessarily expensive. It is also educationally unsound in that it indoctrinates students with the conviction that the only way to really learn anything new is by taking a course in it. Many of the faculty members at Michigan State University, like others elsewhere, do not share this point of view. This is not unnatural, for the proliferate curriculum results much more from faculty self-interest and self-indulgence than it does from student needs.

Educational development at Michigan State University must make some significant attack in this area. Even with heavily increasing numbers of students, effective and economical instructional systems cannot be developed if too many courses result in too many classes with relatively small enrollments.

The Educational Development Program seeks to promote individual and small group learning experiences where these are possible and necessary, and it simultaneously seeks to utilize large group instruction and new media where these are demonstrably effective. Hopefully, better education will result at no increase in cost per student. It is, of course, much too early to say how successful the Educational Development Program will be. Two things are certain: (1) there will be more innovation at Michigan State University, and (2) life will, as in the past, continue to be stimulating or irritating depending on one's predispositions.

Chapter 10

THE UNIVERSITY OF CALIFORNIA, SANTA CRUZ

By Dean E. McHenry*

"Universities easily fall into ruts. Almost every epoch requires a fresh start." These are sentences of Daniel Coit Gilman who founded Johns Hopkins University after a bitter experience with political interference as president of the University of California from 1869 to 1872.

For the first time since it was established 95 years ago the University of California is making two wholly fresh starts. All existing campuses had predecessor institutions. Berkeley grew out of the private College of California in Oakland; Davis was first the University Farm. The San Francisco Medical Center traces its orgins to a private medical school that was donated to the University. UCLA and Santa Barbara began as normal schools that were transferred to the regents. Riverside began as a citrus experiment station. San Diego evolved from the Scripps Institution of Oceanography. But at Irvine and Santa Cruz we are starting from scratch.

The need for another multi-purpose campus in northern California was first indicated publicly in the *Additional Centers* report of 1957. Projections of the State Department of Finance showed that without new campuses the Berkeley campus might be called upon to instruct 27,400 students by 1965 and 35,200 by 1975. The "South Central Coast" counties (San Mateo, Santa Clara, Santa Cruz, San Benito, and Monterey) were designated the appropriate region for a general campus. A new campus program was strongly recommended by the All-University Faculty Conference of 1957. The regents in October, 1957 authorized the new campuses program. The need for

---

*Mr. McHenry is Chancellor of the Santa Cruz Campus of the University of California, Santa Cruz, California.

new campuses was reaffirmed in the Master Plan Survey of 1959-60.

After a thorough site selection study, the regents narrowed the choice for the South Central Coast to two possibilities: the Almaden Valley of Santa Clara County and the Cowell Ranch of Santa Cruz County. In March of 1961 the 2000 acre Cowell site was chosen; the following July the chancellor was appointed and a general allocation of functions was made in the statewide academic plan. In February of 1962 a physical master planning design team of four architects and one landscape architect was chosen.

The provisional academic plan was approved by the regents in November, 1962. A preliminary physical plan was approved in January, 1963 and a final version was adopted in September, 1963. The planning staff moved to Santa Cruz in mid-1962. Construction of buildings began in early 1964.

The terms of reference for the new campuses give considerable latitude for experimentation. The regents in effect told me to build a multi-purpose University campus capable ultimately of accommodating 27,500 students. It was understood, however, that a chancellor or a campus cannot be an island. Neither is free to write the final formula on a blank slate. The University of California, Santa Cruz, belongs to the people of California, whose state constitution lays down some basic rules. The campus is a component part of the University of California system which is governed by rules and policies of the regents and the president. Certain matters are uniform throughout the statewide University; these include student admission standards, staff classification and compensation rates, and dozens of academic and business procedures. On each of the campuses the chancellor is bound to consult on academic matters with representatives of the academic senate which includes virtually all regular faculty members.

The limits on authority that I have mentioned do not seem to me unduly restrictive. The constitution of California makes the University a public trust and grants it considerable independence. The regimen laid down by the regents and the president has permitted existing campuses to develop the finest state university system in the nation. From birth the new campus shares in the endowment, operating budget, and capital outlay moneys of the University of California family. The statewide administration spares us the onerous tasks of representation in Sacramento. The quality control of the academic senate we would want in any case; when the initial faculty is assembled, Santa Cruz will have a senate division of its own.

To dramatize our task we often turn our minds back to the 1890's and the story of the founding of the University of Chicago by William Rainey Harper and of Stanford University by David Starr Jordan. It is certain that we shall not have such peerless leadership, nor will we have private endowments on the order of those provided by the Rockefellers and the Stanfords. We will have, however, some assets they lacked:

1. The sponsorship of a university system that has already achieved much greatness and excellence. We are members of a family of universities. The regents and the central administration and the older campuses stand ready to help but not to interfere so long as the campus operates within the qualitative and procedural limits that have come from the long gestation of University history.

2. The backing of the state of California is a plus factor of immense importance. The current annual supporting budget from the state is the equivalent of the yield of an endowment of more than $4 billion invested at four per cent interest. California has a balanced system of higher education, providing courses of study suitable for the broad spectrum of abilities of its young people in the University of California, the state colleges, and the junior colleges—plus many fine independent institutions.

3. The site on which the new University will be built is excellent; in fact, it is unmatched by any institution I know. Santa Cruz is close to ideal in terms of climate, terrain, and beauty of setting. We hope to construct here something that will be appropriate to the nobility of the site: the views of Monterey Bay, the great forest of redwoods, the varied elevations.

From the time he became president of the University in 1958 Clark Kerr has been placing great stress on innovation and diversity. Those of you who know the Godkin Lectures of last year may recall his "concern with academic conservatism and conformity."

With due respect for the academic traditions of the past, we will strive to do many things quite differently from the conventional. We do not wish to build another Berkeley or UCLA. Instead of imitating, we will ask: "How would they do it if they were free to start over again now?"

Early in the Santa Cruz campus planning President Kerr suggested the one goal that he considered most essential: *try to so organize the campus that it will seem small as it grows large.* The search for an effective response to that challenge has led us to re-examine critically many of the practices of large universities and of small colleges.

In the quest for better ways by which students can learn, we have inquired both into the environments from which they come and into which they go.

The essence of the Santa Cruz plan is to organize instruction in such a way that the advantages of a small college—close instruction, sense of belonging, residential setting—are combined with those of a large university—great scholars, excellent libraries and laboratories, and superior cultural events. We hope in this way to help bridge the gap between the curricular and the co-curricular and to fill in the chasm that so often yawns between students and faculty.

The new campus will begin with a modest input of students and a controlled growth. On opening day in October of 1965 some 60 faculty and 75 non-academic staff members will greet the expected 500 students. It will be deliberate policy to start small and increase slowly. And it is essential that we know the students well from the first, for in that crucial first semester the esprit de corps of the institution may be largely determined.

This new campus will be quite different from its older siblings. Undergraduate instruction will not be en masse. The key to our plan is a series of liberal arts colleges that will average about 600 students, most of whom will "live in." By combining living and learning we expect to reach the whole student and to augment educational effectiveness. Preliminary cost studies indicate that we can operate on the residential college basis at a cost no greater than on the conventional basis.

We define the residential college as an educational unit of a university that combines, to a substantial extent, the functions of an academic unit of administration with co-curricular aspects of undergraduate student life—living, dining, social, athletic, and other. These colleges will be the dominant academic units in the early development of the campus as well as enduring, distinctive features of the ultimate campus organization.

They will take the place of the conventional College of Letters and Science. Within each college will be provided the services not only of the academic dean's office but also those of deans of students, of men, and women. Life in the residential college is expected to be so pervasive that there will be less than the usual level of campus-wide activities and no foreseeable requirement for a large, central student union.

All residential colleges will provide undergraduate liberal arts education but they will vary considerably in shade and emphasis. The provost, by his field and personality, will put a stamp on a college. So will the faculty members attached to the college. Some academic specialization may be predetermined but the way will be left open for a college to adapt or develop new emphases as the years go by.

Undergraduate course offerings will be given in the college whenever fiscally and physically feasible. It is estimated that a student will be able to obtain at least one-half of all his student credit hours through courses given in his college. This will include most of the lower division work and some of the upper division work. In general, an attempt will be made to keep courses small enough for "close" instruction in seminars or tutorials, or large enough to warrant careful preparation by the best lecturers. Courses offered in one college ordinarily will be open to qualified students of other colleges on a space-available basis.

Other courses, particularly those requiring facilities not available in a college, will be offered on a campus-wide basis.

The size of the colleges will vary probably from 250 to 1,000 students. Cowell College, the first and "pilot" unit, is designed for 600 student members of which 400 will "live in" and 200 will commute. To encourage inter-disciplinary cooperation and to minimize particularism there will be no formal departmental organization within the colleges. "Faculty fellows," the academic staff members attached to a particular college, will be joint appointees with the disciplinary group with which they were affiliated. All colleges will have some representation of the principal arts and sciences disciplines.

Cowell College, with 600 student members, will have approximately 30 to 40 faculty fellows and 10 to 12 preceptors (graduate students). To emphasize the importance of the college connection and function, faculty salaries will normally be charged one-half to the college and one-half to the faculty that includes their discipline. Appointments and promotions will be made on recommendations of both (1) the provost of the college on actual or potential contribution to undergraduate teaching and student life and (2) the dean of the faculty on advanced teaching, research, and professional competence. The college will be headed by the provost, a tenure member of the faculty. He and his family will "live in" the college compound in a residence provided by the University. Apartments will also be available for 10 to 12 other fellows and preceptors who are willing to participate in the life of the college most fully.

After there are several colleges, students will probably be assigned to them by a procedure involving a statement of preferences by the applicant and selection by a committee of faculty fellows, using successive rounds until all eligible and available have been chosen.

The colleges will be student-oriented but the atmosphere will be seriously intellectual. The academic program will be heavy, the hours long. A determined effort will be made to reach the "whole" individual and to occupy his entire attention during the academic week.

Ultimately, if the campus grows to 27,500 as anticipated, there will be 15 to 20 of these colleges, plus some professional schools that similarly combine the living-and-learning situation but on the advanced or graduate level.

Although the colleges will adhere to the usual pattern of grades and credits they will make more than usual use of (1) independent study, (2) "pass/fail" grades, and (3) course credit by examination. The colleges will compete with one another in an intramural sports program, the chief means of implementing a campus-wide emphasis on physical fitness for both women and men and a program having the general goal of "many participants, few spectators."

Although the undergraduate colleges must not become so specialized as to be lop-sided and quasi-professional, neither can they be allowed to be simply general liberal arts units with no personality or distinctiveness of their own. Differentiation among the colleges will be induced by having different (1) provosts; (2) faculties; (3) student bodies; (4) location, architecture, and facilities; (5) traditions and conditions of growth; (6) sizes; and (7) possibly in some cases sex—coeducation, men's colleges, and women's colleges.

Without losing its common devotion to liberal education or denying the right of any other college to have majors in the field, a college might develop a special curricular emphasis. A college also might acquire a flavor or flair by the infusion of professional school staff (such as business) as faculty fellows, or by concentration in it of those academic staff members constituting the "team" for a particular research specialty (such as genetics).

Cowell College, which will be quite general in the beginning, will later emphasize the humanities. The second college will have a strong public affairs and social sciences slant. It will have 700 students of whom a higher proportion will be commuters than in Cowell. The third college will emphasize science in the manner of Churchill College, Cambridge, and Harvey Mudd, Claremont; it will have 500 student members. We plan to hold to a maximum of 50 per cent the proportion of students majoring in the area of emphasis of a college; thus the science college will have no more than one-half of its students specializing in science and mathematics.

All colleges will be undergraduate liberal arts units; all will receive both freshmen and transfers with advanced standing. Some professional schools may use certain of the "collegiate" features suggested for residential colleges, but the distinction must be clear between the goals of the two. The college is in the liberal arts tradition; it seeks breadth of preparation, reserving for later the specialization that will train directly for the professions. The professional school, on the other hand,

places less emphasis on breadth and concentrates on the technical studies that lead to the expertness necessary to immediate
practice of a profession.

For a variety of reasons it will be necessary to organize
campus-wide academic units that cut across college lines. To
justify the name of university and to attract a faculty worthy
of such an institution, graduate work and research must be
important considerations from the beginning. In many fields
distinction is unlikely to be achieved without a critical minimum of colleagues who associate frequently and who have access to appropriate facilities—laboratory, library, and other.
Groupings by discipline are also needed to fix the responsibility
for determining professional competence, for judging the quality of research work, and for guiding graduate students. Contacts by discipline with colleagues in other institutions and in
learned societies—regional, national, and international—are desirable to place students, to find outlets for creative work, and
to secure informed reactions to one's ideas and experiments.

The broad grouping of the arts and sciences initially will be:
humanities, social sciences, and natural sciences. The humanities will embrace history, philosophy, languages and literatures,
and the fine arts. The social sciences will cover anthropology,
sociology, economics, geography, government, and psychology.
The natural sciences will combine the biological—botany and
zoology—with the physical—chemistry, mathematics, and physics. Unique results in teaching and research should come from
interdisciplinary cooperation fostered by such a combination.

Ultimately the arts and sciences groupings may become
schools operating mainly on the graduate levels. For the initial
period it will suffice if they are organized as "faculties." In any
case they should be composed of all members of the academic
senate holding appointments in relevant fields and they should
be headed by deans who share power and responsibility with
the deans of the colleges in initiating and recommending decisions on academic personnel matters, including appointments
and promotions.

Typically a new academic position will appear in the budget
on a joint basis, for example, faculty fellow of Cowell College
and assistant professor of history. The deans and fellows of

Cowell, on one hand, and the dean and faculty of the school, on the other, will have mutual responsibility for finding and recommending the appropriate candidate for the post.

The school or faculty may ultimately be further subdivided into campus-wide departments for convenience of administration. In the initial years, however, formation of departments will be deferred for policy and pedagogical reasons. Until the colleges are firmly rooted and the character of the undergraduate instructional function is firmly established, it appears ill-advised to set up conventional departments. The early years should be a period of ferment and cross-pollinating among the disciplines. Particularism at that stage might lead to de-emphasis on undergraduate education. If this took place the college might end up being little more than dormitories with occasional tutorials.

The statewide academic plan mentions the possibility that Santa Cruz might develop schools of engineering and business and that it might eventually receive, by transfer from Berkeley, the well-established School of Forestry. Other possible specialties that might affect the professional school alignment are landscape architecture, conservation of natural resources, and recreation.

In addition to the specialties suggested above there is interest in other possibilities which might begin as informal pockets of strength in the colleges and later emerge as centers or institutes. Among those under consideration are language and linguistics, South Pacific studies, social psychology, and applied mathematics.

The library will be the intellectual heart of Santa Cruz campus. From the beginning it will be molded by four formative influences:

1. A centrally located undergraduate collection of 50,000 to 75,000 carefully selected volumes is likely to be available on opening day.

2. The residential colleges will have substantial libraries and sizable reading rooms; their collections of 10,000 to 15,000 volumes each will be composed mainly of duplicate books, reference works, and paperbacks.

3. The emphasis on humanities and social sciences will re-

quire extraordinary support for the library to build up research collections in the various areas of specialization.

4. There will be available, through inter-library loans and travel-by-readers, the vast resources of the Berkeley and other University libraries. It is proposed to operate an inter-campus bus daily from Santa Cruz and to encourage faculty members and graduate students who have need for materials from the Berkeley and San Francisco collections to use them fully and frequently.

As soon as the library building is completed in 1966 it should be a central focus of faculty research work in the humanities and social sciences. Carrels and other facilities will be provided for the convenience of faculty and graduate students. As the campus grows and the need for quick delivery of materials to far corners of the campus arises, pneumatic and other methods may be developed instead of permitting branch libraries.

Although initial emphasis will be given to undergraduate work the graduate function is of great importance and will not be minimized. Graduate students begin on opening day and by 1975 probably will exceed 15 per cent of total enrollments. It is necessary that the faculty, both initial and subsequent, be recruited with due recognition that it must do more than teach undergraduates.

Doctoral programs will be offered in the first years only in disciplines selected for early emphasis. They must be supported by exceptional faculty strength and excellent library and laboratory facilities. To secure well-rounded guidance and to provide additional quality control, faculty members from other campuses of the University will be invited to sit as members of Ph.D. committees.

The latest developments in communication and programed learning will have a prominent part both in internal teaching and in external relations. Television cables will be built in and among the major buildings and closed circuit television will make it possible for a single lecturer or a special event to reach classes in the various colleges without convening all students in a single large auditorium. The campus may also have a future with open circuit TV.

In making projections of teaching staff several considerations must be borne in mind. The all-University faculty/student ratio of 1 to 16 and teaching staff/student ratio of 1 to 12 will be achieved within the first ten years of operation.

To determine the appropriate distribution of faculty by rank various arguments and experiences must be considered. There is wide agreement that Riverside started too overweighted with junior staff and insufficient in the tenure ranks. On the other extreme, San Diego has emphasized senior appointments and has built a staff of distinction rapidly. To repeat the San Diego approach would require funds that are not likely to be available and would aggravate the concentration in tenure ranks already so great at the Berkeley and Los Angeles campuses. Consequently a middle road that provides a majority of junior appointments but a strong representation in the upper ranks will be followed.

The Santa Cruz faculty probably will be drawn mainly from the leading graduate schools as are faculty members of other campuses of the University. An effort will be made, however, to recruit some academic staff from three other promising sources: other campuses of the University, retired professors, and women.

There will be special concern at Santa Cruz for faculty housing. The college plan requires close association of faculty fellows with the many activities of their colleges. For this reason provision will be made for some who are without children to live in college facilities. Others should be given the opportunity to live close by if they wish.

We are spending much time and treasure on the physical arrangements to serve the Santa Cruz campus. We justify this by citing Winston Churchill who said at the time of the rebuilding of the House of Commons: "We mold our buildings and later they mold us." The site for the campus is three miles long and one mile wide. The academic core of library, laboratories, and other central facilities will be built near the geographic center. Residential colleges will occupy knolls on the east and west sides. Science research installations will be placed in the north. The south will be left largely open, with some scattered professional schools and public service facilities. The great forest permits a considerable variation of architectural treatment; eight different architectural firms have so far been commissioned to do the first nine projects.

The most crucial prerequisite to accomplishing the goals of the Santa Cruz campus is the selection of a faculty that is able and dedicated. No one has stated this imperative better than Gilman at his inaugural as president of the University of California:

> It is on the faculty that the building of a university depends. It is not the site, nor the apparatus, nor the library, nor the Regents, which draws the scholars; it is a body of scholars, skilled in their specialties, eminent in their calling, loving to teach. Such a body will make a university anywhere.

We have most of the essentials in prospect: a fine site, a building program underway, a library collection already reaching the size of the Lamont, and a governing board and a state-wide administration giving full support. Our main tasks now, without neglecting or belittling the other responsibilities, are to lay out an academic program and seek out a staff that can put life and vigor into it.

Chapter 11

MONTEITH COLLEGE OF WAYNE STATE UNIVERSITY

By Woodburn O. Ross*

Monteith College occupies a most unusual position in American higher education. It is a small, degree-granting liberal arts college on a huge university campus and it exists side-by-side with a conventional liberal arts college of more than 10,000 students. It enjoys precisely the same autonomy as does its larger brother: that is, it is given its own budget by the central administration of Wayne State University; employs its own faculty, who teach only in Monteith; and in general determines its own educational policies, restricted only by those broad policies of the entire University which apply to all colleges. Thus Monteith does not determine its own salary structure. The salary structure of the University is devised by the central administration and, for the most part, is the same for all colleges. On the other hand Monteith does fix its own promotion policy and behaves as it sees fit with relation to class size, teaching load, and requirements for graduation. It is free in these matters within the limitation of its budget.

The University established Monteith in the hope that this new unit would explore ways of dealing with two vexing problems—the perennial one of the general education of the undergraduate and the developing one of the most appropriate organization and administration of the increasing masses of undergraduate students appearing on the campus, a particularly difficult problem in a commuter university such as Wayne State. It conveys, perhaps, a false impression to refer to these as problems as if they were single and, it might be, simple.

---

*Mr. Ross is Dean of Monteith College, Wayne State University, Detroit, Michigan.

Rather each is a closely related group of problems, a syndrome, the various elements of which are related to one another in a highly complex fashion.

The generosity of the Ford Foundation provided a total of $725,000 for the planning and initiation of the College.

I shall discuss first Monteith's operation in this broad area of undergraduate general education and shall begin negatively by exploring our reasons for *not* doing certain things.

We decided that the new organization ought not to be a part of the existing College of Liberal Arts. We made this decision despite the fact that many of the general education programs which we looked at, heard about, or read about were parts of the conventional college. The difficulty seemed to lie in the very nature of the contemporary colleges of liberal arts.

These institutions are indeed enjoying a period of immense vitality. Their faculties are genuinely imaginative and creative particularly in the areas of the social and natural sciences. They have a sense of mission; they are discoverers. They publish. The professors in these faculties, devoted to the cultivation of their disciplines, quite properly draw a major portion of their sense of professional accomplishment from the additions which they make to the body of knowledge comprehended by their academic disciplines. Their primary professional loyalties appear to be, not to their universities or to the courses they teach, but to the disciplines which are national and international in scope. Administrators share with their faculties the admiration for research and they in turn compete with one another with regard to the numbers of famous and highly productive scholars they can induce to join the institutions of which they are executive officers. Needless to say, it is the rule in most liberal arts colleges for the promotion of a faculty member to depend to a very large extent upon his publications. The officer responsible for recommending all promotions in one of our major universities told me last summer that before he acted favorably upon a man he asked himself what the man's discipline would have been like if the man had never lived. In such an environment as I am describing graduate students are much sought after. On the one hand they, the most advanced students, those closest to the outer boundaries of knowledge in their field, themselves actively engaged in research, confer prestige upon their professors; on the other, they are frequently of direct and immediate help to their professors' own investigations.

I submit that there is a great virtue in the system I have just been describing. It is the best system which our culture has produced for intellectual discovery within the universities—perhaps the best within the entire culture itself. It stimulates intellectual excitement; it generates an atmosphere of intellectual alertness. It does much to make possible the technology that supports our millions of people; it provides a framework for our gaining fruitful insights into our social organization and behavior; it opens pathways into the world of the arts. It places a premium on certain kinds of creation; and the man who has ceased to create has become moribund.

But I submit also that this academic climate may not be one in which most undergraduate students, particularly the underclassmen, can be expected to flourish. The faculty member who devotes his time to his undergraduate students, even though very successfully, runs a grave risk, as we all know, of retiring as an associate professor with an associate professor's salary. Few men, even among those inspired to teach, care to run this risk for themselves and their families. Such a man has little hope of improving his lot by moving to another campus. Even if he has made some reputation by his teaching it is likely to be strictly local and it is therefore unlikely that any other school will know of his accomplishments and offer him a post. Undergraduates in our liberal arts colleges tend, therefore, to be taught by professors compelled by the deepest demands of the system under which they work to devote much, in most cases probably the major portion, of their energies to research—and research which frequently has no direct discernible relationship to the needs of undergraduate students. The underclassmen tend, of course, to be even worse off than juniors and seniors for they fall into the hands of teaching assistants, graduate students who, indeed, no matter how well they might teach under other circumstances must here and now devote their time and attention to their dissertations under pain of failing before they really start.

There are, of course, exceptions to the processes I have just described and I wish to recognize the fact. But in general the miniature I have drawn is, I believe, a recognizable if restricted copy of the real world.

It was in part such considerations as these which led us to reject the notion of existing within the College of Liberal Arts and operating under its policies and within its climate. For we were about to set up a formal general education curriculum and it was our opinion that the new, synthetic general courses which we were to plan would place maximal demands upon the teaching abilities of our staff. We proposed, therefore, to reward good teaching above all else—to reward it with salary and promotion. We wanted our people to see themselves as primarily battling for the minds of their students, as ushering them into the world of ideas, as enabling them to sense, at least, the wild excitement of the life of the mind. From our beginnings we preferred the question "What would this man's students have missed had he never lived?" to "What would his discipline have lacked?" In short, we did not wish our staff to compete with colleagues in the conventional disciplines under rules drawn up by the College of Liberal Arts.

We did not, however, turn our backs upon the necessity that our people create. As we saw it, creation was of the very essence. But what they must create—or help create—was new, synthetic academic disciplines. We organized ourselves into three divisions called the Science of Society, Natural Science, and Humanistic Studies. We did not, for example, try to design courses which would give a student a short introduction to economics, another to political science, another to sociology, another to social psychology. Such introductions, we believed, were bound to be superficial and intellectually stultifying— and in any case they were pointless. Our purpose was to place before the student the finest fruits of the reflection and research which our culture had produced. The questions we asked ourselves were not on the order of "How can we teach a little political science?" but on that of "How can we lead a student to entertain the most intellectually sophisticated ideas which humanity has achieved about man as a social being?"—quite without regard, insofar as possible, to the discipline which produced them. Approaching our task thus, we felt it necessary to begin hiring staff members and putting them to work several months before we admitted our first class.

All were to be engaged in research; they had to be. But the hoped-for end of the research was not the discovery of a new fact or a fresh insight. It was the isolation and organization of the ideas and procedures which were to make up our courses. An early discovery was that two of the staffs, at least, would have to produce some of their own texts. They set to work and have never stopped. Indeed, because the courses are under constant revision, members of the Monteith faculty would have published locally some thirty volumes, principally collections of readings for Monteith students. Here is research intimately connected with the process of teaching undergraduates; research which does not set up within a professor a tension between teaching students and carrying on activities somewhat more likely to produce fame, advancement, and three or more meals a day; research through which a man develops as a productive scholar at the same time he keeps his eyes on his students.

Another kind of research undertaken within the College has had to do with the students' use of the library. A grant by the Office of Education made possible the setting-up of a program which sought out means of uniting library staff members with each instructional staff, deriving much of the intellectual development of students from the library and thus making it highly functional in the eyes of the members of our community—of making the library, in short, the center of the learning process which it should and frequently may not be. Here again is undergraduate-oriented research, immediately influential on the college scene. I may remark in passing that as a result of this library experiment the class upon which it was visited gained a campus-wide reputation for sophistication in the use of the University library such as I have never seen before and the library itself, complex as it is, became in the minds of large numbers of the students the usable undergraduate tool which it can be. Our college is now seeking a further grant by which to develop a permanent library-orientation of the college community.

I turn now to another major matter though one which can

be treated more briefly than the last. Most structured general education programs, I believe, are related to the students' first and second years in college. This organization, I think, is derived principally from the 19th Century German system in which general studies were considered less demanding than, and suitably preliminary to, specialization. There are at least two serious objections to adapting such a structure to 20th Century American colleges and universities. In the first place, the movement for organized general education in the United States is a direct result of the 20th-century explosion of knowledge and the necessity of putting this knowledge in the service of society in the most complete and effective way. General studies have thus become extremely demanding intellectually and cannot be handled adequately if presented only to the most immature minds on the campus scene. They must command the attention of juniors and seniors as well as of freshmen and sophomores. Secondly, the presentation of general courses in the beginning collegiate years leads to the false and dangerous conception that they are properly to be regarded as introductions to this or that. In fact they are not good introductions to anything except life itself. They are independent, synthetic academic disciplines, responsive to intellectual needs and now being born.

They cannot, however, take the place of the more conventional specialized disciplines such as physics, economics, philosophy, history. We in Monteith, at least, do not believe that either the generalist or the specialist has the complete answer to contemporary academic needs; consequently we arrange our curriculum so that a student seeking a Monteith degree spends approximately half his time during each of his four undergraduate years in our general courses and about half his time in the conventional department of his choice in the College of Liberal Arts.

Each Monteith student is required to take the basic sequence of courses in each of the Monteith divisions. The basic sequences in the Science of Society and in Humanistic Studies are each five quarters long; that in Natural Science is six. The student begins the sequence in Science of Society and that in Natural Science as a freshman. He begins the sequence in

Humanistic Studies in the middle of his sophomore year and finishes at the end of his junior year. In his final year he takes his Senior Colloquium, a capstone of his Monteith work, and writes an elaborate senior essay. Monteith also offers certain interdisciplinary elective courses based upon portions of the material covered in the so-called basic courses. All this constitutes the general education portion of his curriculum. In the rest of his time the student is free to specialize usually taking courses in his specialty in the conventional College of Liberal Arts. Any student has the time in which to fulfill the entrance requirements of the professional school of graduate department of his choice. As a matter of fact, much to our astonishment we have found that 80 per cent of last year's graduates are now in a professional or graduate school.

Finally, before I close my discussion of the Monteith curriculum and structure, I wish a say a word about our development of a formal program of independent study for our students. When we were planning the College we were concerned, as many professors are, at the dependence of the American undergraduate upon formal instruction and assignments, at his inability or unwillingness to seize an intellectual initiative, give rein to his curiosity, plan in large part his own intellectual development. The thought occurred to us that we had, in the five-and-six-quarter basic courses which we were planning, a possible way of attacking this problem. With some misgivings we decided· to require each student to take the final quarter of one of these courses—he was left free to choose which one—by what we called semi-independent study. I must explain here certain matters relating to these courses. Each meets four times a week, twice a week in large groups for lectures and twice a week in small discussion groups. A student's instructor is the man in charge of his discussion group. These are very small: 12 students to a freshman section, 16 to a sophomore, and 20 to a junior section. (Since we have both very large and very small classes, we have developed some tentative opinions on the vexed question of class size; but I shall touch upon this matter later.) The lectures are open to everybody, staff members of our College, staff members of other colleges, any students whatsoever; and we never take attendance to determine whether students enrolled in the course have duly shown up.

Now a student choosing to fulfill his semi-independent study requirement by, let us say, Natural Science 233, is denied access to any discussion section in that course. Since anybody at all may attend the lectures, he is of course free to go. But since he is in no section he has no instructor to turn to for help. He must do the same reading and thinking and take the same examinations as his fellows. But in fulfilling the requirements of the course he is necessarily left very much on his own. This method of inducting a student into independent study appealed to us principally for this reason: since the requirement called for him to take the final segment of a basic course by semi-independent study he was not thrown on his own before he had spent at least a year and a quarter in the course he was to tackle independently. Under instruction he would have been trained in method and would have gained momentum in the exploration of the area in question which should afford him background and at least some self-confidence.

Experience has shown that whereas a student approaches his independent work with trepidation similar to that with which most of us would approach a dive into very cold water, he can nevertheless do what is asked of him. As a matter of fact, the independent students tend to make slightly higher final grades than their colleagues who are under formal instruction. This fact, however, is probably not very significant since the student chooses the area in which he will first study independently and presumably he chooses that area in which he has the most talent. In his senior year, as I have said, each student writes a Senior Essay and takes the Senior Colloquium. In both these exercises he is largely independent; both are in a sense follow-ups of earlier semi-independent work. And between the time of his successfully taking his first hurdle in independent work and his maturity as a senior he is likely to elect at least some tutorials or undergraduate seminars in the College. In these undertakings he is given ample opportunity to develop intellectually with minimal supervision. In other words, once a student has convinced himself that he does have independent intellectual capacity he is anxious to exercise it.

Our independent study program thus depends at its beginning upon the structure of the curriculum which makes it possible for us to ask a student to take work without assigning him an instructor only after he has had more than a year's experience in the sequence in which he will work independently.

I turn now to the second of the two principal aspects of Monteith which I wish to discuss. Monteith was planned as a small college offering its work in small classes. I shall first briefly discuss class size.

We of the College have not yet attempted formally to determine what the size of classes should be but we have developed certain definite hunches about the matter. We distrust conclusions that students can be taught as well in large classes as in small because we are not sure that the possibilities of the small class are always clearly enough understood and exploited. If I have before me 200 or 500 students—a large class—and lecture at them I can to some extent both instruct and amuse. If I take 20 or 40 students and talk to them I can perhaps behave a little more informally and so alter the atmosphere of the class a bit; but fundamentally, I am still doing the same thing as I was to the class of 200 or 500 and I think that I shall get almost identical results. In other words, my own experience tells me—and I believe that the experience of my colleagues in the College tells them the same—that class size *in itself* is not significant. It is what happens in the classroom that counts. The possibilities for effective teaching offered by the really small discussion group are very great; if they are not used, however, the advantages offered are of course lost. In a small class, one of about a dozen students, the initiation of a genuine dialogue usually becomes possible, one between students and teacher, one among students. In such a dialogue ideas are viewed from various points of view, their implications are explored, they give rise to fresh ideas. We all know that a tool untried is a tool unknown. The same is true in the world of ideas. Unless ideas are used in discussion to build an edifice of thought, unless they are manipulated, amplified, forced into new shapes, they really remain largely unknown and can only be parroted. A class lectured at, unless groups within it set up their own dialogue independently, does, I think, tend to parrot. A class taught very differently, by the initiation and development of significant discussion, is much more likely really to affect the student.

Partly for economic reasons Monteith does, in each basic course as I have said, make use of both methods. Information can be and is conveyed in lectures; it becomes alive, meaningful, useful in the discussion groups.

I believe it is the opinion of most members of the staff that lecturing is a good deal easier than initiating a good discussion. As a distinguished visitor to our college recently said, with perhaps some exaggeration, "You can wind up anybody from behind to give a good lecture." But the initiation of good discussion, training of members of a class in systematic discussion techniques—these things require in a very high degree the practice of an art by the teacher. Occasionally he may find himself in a really impossible situation, one in which the chances of registration have produced a class of a dozen or more students most of whom are reticent, not accustomed to verbalize, not easily interested in the subject-matter of the course. Under such circumstances a deliberate re-shuffle of students in sections of the course meeting at that hour might be in order.

Just as we believe that small classes which engage in constant dialogue are necessary if the minds of undergraduates are to be caught, so we believe that small colleges forming self-conscious communities serve education better than large ones. A student lost in a mass is likely to be a student who turns mechanical in his academic work, grinds out his assignments as best he may, and finds vital significance in sub-groups, perhaps social, which he spontaneously helps form, or finding them already existing, joins. In the urban street-car universities such as Wayne State, which very many undergraduates attend today, small academic units would seem to be particularly necessary. If the culture of the University is to compete with the culture of the neighborhood or of the job it must manifestly exist and attract. It does not manifestly exist for most students going from class to class to job.

Wayne State University has a large student center at which meals are served, spots for study exist, and certain university-wide social events occur. Monteith maintains its own student center, a large, rather tumbled-down former residence of the kind by which the campus is surrounded. Here students are in charge. Within the framework of general University policy they are free to govern the use of the building. Here a student government has its headquarters; here invited lecturers speak; here occur informal bull sessions; here social events are held; here ideas are discussed. In connection with the last point I call attention to the closely-knit structure of the basic Monteith curriculum. All freshmen are encountering similar ideas at the same time in the social and natural sciences; all sophomores, similar ideas at the same time in these courses and, after the first quarter, in humanities; all juniors, in humanities. This situation offers great opportunity for the development of informal, spontaneous, intellectual discussions at the student center. We hope, in short, that the center contributes to an important extent in the development of a true small-college community on the huge Wayne State campus.

The Monteith student body is recruited in a rather complex fashion and is, as nearly as we can manage, a cross-section of Wayne State undergraduates. We are quite deliberately not an honors college. Or perhaps it would be more accurate to say that we deliberately do not recruit honors students but we hope that we graduate honors students.

What kind of results, you may ask, has Monteith achieved? It is too early to attempt definitive answers to this immensely complex question. The College has thus far graduated only one class. For the past two years, however, thanks to a grant of $137,000 from the Office of Education, we have been conducting a program study which should have some tentative answers ready for publication within another year. For the present, let me cite only two facts which we have available. Some of you are doubtless familiar with the College Characteristics Index, a new instrument designed to do just what its name suggests—describe the characteristics of a college. It is not a test of cognition. One large portion of this Index, to me the most interesting portion, is designed to assess intellectual climates. We administered the entire instrument to our students. If the results are to be believed, the intellectual climate of Monteith is very salubrious indeed. Our score here was well beyond a sigma above the arithmetic mean of the scores of the other colleges using the Index; it put us in very exclusive company. We also administered the area portion of the Graduate Record Examination to all graduating seniors last year. Measured in terms of national norms, their median scores in the social sciences fell in the 72nd percentile, in the humanities in the 74th percentile, and in the natural sciences in the 78th percentile.

Chapter 12

PROPOSED NEW COLLEGE FOR THE FLORIDA STATE UNIVERSITY

By R. R. OGLESBY*

During the past eight months seven members of the faculty and administration have been drawn together by their common concern about undergraduate education at Florida State University. What factors generated this concern? First, with increasing enrollments there has been a growing tendency toward impersonal treatment of students, a hiatus between students and faculty. Second, as the physical plant grows larger and facilities are strained to their limits the uses of individual units have become increasingly disjunctive. Classrooms are for lectures only, dormitories for sleep and socializing, libraries for reading, and faculty offices for consultation or off limits. Third, and perhaps most disturbing, is the artificial separation of areas of knowledge and the increasing insularity between schools and departments.

Our challenge has been and will continue to be the breaching of the psychological gap between students and faculty, the physical gap between dormitory and classroom, and the intellectual gap between art and zoology.

We are intrigued by the prospect of a college which will evoke a much greater degree of identification of the student as well as a significantly greater commitment to learning; a col-

---

*Mr. Oglesby is Dean of Students, Florida State University, Tallahassee, Florida. This chapter is a composite of the thinking of the members of the Florida State University Committee on an Experimental College as of the end of the academic year 1963-64. Members of the Committee are: the Assistant Dean of Faculties, Dean of the Graduate School, Dean of the College of Arts and Sciences, Dean of the Library School, the University Librarian, the Head of the Department of Higher Education, and the Dean of Students. The President of the University has met frequently with the Committee in its deliberations.

lege that will develop techniques for synthesizing knowledge without sacrificing education in depth within specific areas of knowledge or even within highly specialized topics; a college that will break from the traditions of 55-minute classes, credit hour requirements, or grade point averages carried three digits beyond the decimal point.

We concur in the belief that the academic program should deal with knowledge as a continuous, interrelated process throughout the student's career. We believe that daily participation in academic discussions is as essential as are daily requirements for effective reading and writing.

We found ourselves in agreement with a recent report published by the Hazen Foundation which pointed out that something fundamental must be changed in American higher education if we are to educate youth to meet the challenge of a rapidly changing world.

If liberal education is to meet the requirements of a new kind of world it must undergo one of those fundamental overhauls that have kept it alive for centuries. There is need for more than adding a course here and there, more than repackaging of old courses. There must be a reformulation of purpose. The great humanistic philosophy in liberal learning must be translated into 20th Century terms. . . .

Aims and Purposes

We make the assumption that the goal of the University must also be the goal of the College. According to the last University self-study completed in 1962, the University's primary goal "is to establish an intellectual climate in which students develop respect for truth and excitement in discovery." If this result is to be achieved certain steps appear obvious. The College must truly be student-centered. Experience demonstrates that only by this means can a proper cultural climate for learning be established. The development of the student for high achievement in community life must ultimately stem from self-discipline. So the students must be given major responsibility for control of their personal and community life. There is no other way by which responsible students can be developed than by giving them responsibility.

Not only will we give the student much responsibility for his own conduct and for the operation of the College, but we propose also to take that "modicum of curiosity and wonder" possessed by each student and proceed to develop a thoughtful, critical approach to learning rather than the mere accumulation of facts. We will expect students to look beyond facts to meaning, beyond the force of gravity in the fall of an apple to fruiting and decay as a process of life. Facts may be accumulated for utilitarian purposes. But man's eternal quest as to who he is, why he is here, or what is the meaning of faith and life and truth cannot be answered by accumulation of data alone.

Since every good poem or short story or novel, every enduring painting, every great piece of music, every lasting sculpture addresses itself to the question "Who am I?," it will be particularly appropriate for a college which lays stress on the humanities to concern itself with meanings.

Early in a consideration of the aims and purposes the question arose as to whether this College will be established as an experimenting one which would touch directly only a very small proportion of the student body of the University and which might largely become obsessed with achieving its own ends and perpetuating itself. Should it be an "honors college," not only with intellectually favored students, but also with a faculty favored in instructional load, in student-teacher ratio, and in budget? Such a college offers pleasant and exciting possibilities.

But on reflection it was realized that a larger and more difficult task lay ahead for the College if it is truly to serve the best interests and most pressing needs of a large state university. It must provide an answer to the great question facing all large state universities: can quantity higher education possess intimacy and quality?

The answer to that central question inevitably led us to conclude that no college founded on Utopian dreams, however pleasant and inviting, can be the answer for an institution such as the Florida State University which is committed to the education of a large number of young people of the state.

We concluded that ours must be a prototype college, so managed and operated that it will serve as the first of a series of colleges around which other parts of our undergraduate program can be organized. If it succeeds, its experience will be directed toward involving as much of the total undergraduate program as appropriate. It must be a pilot college rather than a token effort to distract attention from the weaknesses of existing undergraduate programs.

Once the decision to establish a prototype college was made, certain other decisions followed. Faculty-student ratio and per student costs must fall within University norms. Students must be considered as members of the University student body, not as a group apart.

The Organization

The organizational chart of the College will be simple because there will be little administrative hierarchy. While the College is expected to be an integral part of the University, yet it should have sufficient autonomy to develop its own set of rules, procedures, and policies that are necessary for fulfilling its purposes. This applies to both academic and social regulations, as well as to its budget.

The principal administrative officer will report to the academic vice president and through him to the president. Subject to the approval of the faculty senate, the College will develop a separate set of academic regulations. It will have appropriate representation on the faculty senate. Insofar as possible, the College will have autonomy in internal self-government, and the students will be expected to have substantial responsibility for management of the affairs of the College. The College will depend on the University for many service functions such as admissions, record keeping, financial aid, maintenance, food services, purchasing, health services, and the like. It will develop its own intramural athletic program within the total program of the University.

The Faculty

The faculty for the College must not only be competent specialists but also be able to relate the specialties of their discipline to the whole spectrum of human knowledge. They must have a passion for teaching and a contagious enthusiasm for their profession. They must be both learners and teachers, working with students as senior partners in the enterprise of education.

It is assumed that the College will have approximately the same student-teacher ratio established in the University. Since little specialization of functions will exist in the College, the positions normally assigned to administrative services and counseling will be assigned to people who are teacher-administrators, teacher-counselors, teacher-researchers, teacher-librarians. Study and research will continue to be important functions as they always are for the good professor, but they will assume importance because, in fact, they so affect directly the quality of the instruction. Every person connected with the College will be expected to be first and primarily a teacher—not only in the broadest meaning of that word but in the very narrow and specific sense of meeting with students in a learning situation.

It is proposed that some of the faculty in the College will be permanently assigned full-time, both administratively and budget-wise, to the College. Others will be selected from the general faculty of the University on a lend-lease basis for periods of a term, a year, or longer. Some faculty may teach part-time in the College and part-time in the University. It is expected that at least 40 per cent of the faculty will come from the humanities—English, philosophy, art, music, and languages —since the major emphasis for this particular College will be in that area. About 30 per cent will come from the social sciences and the remainder from the natural sciences, with a smattering from the needed specialties such as library science.

What are the qualities which will be expected in the faculty? In brief—good teaching! This means they must be competent scholars in their disciplines, respected and admired as persons rather than feared as authorities; loyal to the basic premises on which the College is established; inclined to be philosophical and general rather than narrow as specialists; willing to accept and encourage a large measure of student independence of thought and action. If there is one hallmark of the good teacher, it is the quality of enthusiasm—enthusiasm for his subject but more importantly enthusiasm for his students. Chaucer said of his teacher, "Gladly would he learn and gladly teach."

Since the College will be a center for learning, it will be a place dedicated to the quest for truth and insights, a quest which must involve the teacher as much as it does the student. The teacher in this College must put himself in the position of a learner, and in this role he shares a companionship with his students. In the necessary relationships between students and teachers in the proposed College a companionship of learning must exist.

When professor and student accept their common ignorance, they stand humbled before the vast potentials for further explorations within the universe. Teachers must explore with their students, even along paths which for the teachers are already well charted. When both student and teacher reach the boundary line where knowledge for both stops and ignorance for both begins, it is at this point that the rich rewards of intellectual companionship truly begin.

We have been cautioned that this commitment will be too demanding on the teachers and that faculty exhaustion will soon take place. We believe we can find scholars dedicated enough to take that risk. However, there are certain factors which will tend to minimize the pressures on the faculty. Since lectures will be held to a minimum, not only can these few be prepared with great care, but also actually much time of the faculty will be released for participation in group discussions and team teaching. Since one of the major responsibilities of the student will be his own self-education through independent study, the arduous role of the teacher as a taskmaster is thereby diminished.

The Curriculum

Some general principles have been laid down as guidelines for curriculum development. The objectives of the College will constitute its academic charter. Once the objectives are established and promulgated, the curriculum must be so fashioned as faithfully to fulfill the aims and purposes agreed upon. For instance, it is said that the College will involve the student totally both in and out of the classroom. The curriculum should then be conceived as everything which happens to the student. Curricular and co-curricular activities will be looked on as two coordinate aspects of a single program. Much of the outside class activities will in fact constitute laboratory-learning situations.

The curriculum should be organized into a flexible calendar. The hours of the day, days of the week, and months of the academic year must serve the student and assist him in his academic goals. Neither the students nor the College can afford to follow slavishly a made-in-advance inflexible time schedule. If a visiting poet or a significant national or international event is of consuming interest for a day or two, then all thoughts and energies will be turned in that direction.

The curriculum shall provide for major emphasis on independent study. Library resources, audio-visual materials, programed learning devices, radio, and television will have appropriate roles to play to the extent that they augment the student's independent study and are not allowed to impersonalize the learning process.

The major emphasis will be in the humanistic studies. It is not proposed that this first College serve the needs of all students but rather those students already oriented toward the humanities. There will be little or no place in the curriculum for the professional emphasis. Rather the curriculum should seek to integrate and synthesize the best of the past and the present in the liberal tradition. Past will give understanding to the present, and both past and present will give perspective to the future.

The curriculum will be designed to cause the student to respond positively to the creative expressions of the human spirit and to be an active participant in creative endeavors. The student will do more than appreciate and enjoy; he will be expected to engage in creative activity—writing, painting, composing, or performing.

The curriculum will be so constructed as to assist the student in the development of ethical values and spiritual resources. An educated person recognizes the ethical values and spiritual foundations of human existence, and in his search for values he is characterized by the same humble search for truth that marks his search in other areas of human experience.

A high level command of one modern foreign language will

be expected of the students by having this one language diligently studied throughout the College years. The graduate of the College should be able to read the language rapidly and understand it well, to write skillfully in the language, to understand the spoken language, and to speak the language fluently.

The areas of instruction will be broadly conceived; courses arranged in neat packages of a specified number of semester hours will be avoided. Rather the three areas of learning—humanities, the social sciences, and the natural sciences—will form the cornerstones of the curriculum, and progressions in these fields will be designated in annual increments such as Humanities I, Humanities II, Humanities III, and the like.

Athletic, social, and recreational activities will be so designed as to complement the in-class aspects of instruction rather than distract from them. Under such an arrangement intramural athletics should be far more important than intercollegiate athletics. But all activities, whether athletic, social, or recreational, must be designed to augment the aims and purposes of the College.

In summary, educational methods in the College will be dramatically different. It is anticipated that there will be no rigid, inflexible, lockstep curriculum through which every student must pass. There will be no formal courses, no required number of hours of credit, and no grades. Every day will be viewed as a total learning experience for each student who will be in daily close association with several stimulating faculty members and will get to know them intimately. The College will conduct a program of instruction and discussion which will evolve from a consideration of origins of the universe and the history of mankind to a focus upon contemporary issues and the problems of the future. Since all students will be expected to write and speak extensively, faculty members will be engaged in a continuing discourse with each student.

Students

Students will meet the same basic admission requirements of high school grade average and ability scores as other Florida State University students. We anticipate that students will represent a cross-section of the intellectual ability of the total student population of the University. In addition, through personal interview it should be ascertained whether the prospective student has all or some of the following qualifications: is inquisitive; has read a number of serious books; is reasonably articulate in both oral and written expression; is inwardly motivated; has talents and skills in special fields of endeavor such as music, art, politics, writing, acting, or in demonstrated leadership; can become enthusiastic about an idea, a new truth, or a new thing of beauty. In other words, qualitative factors will be employed so that we may select a lively, thoughtful, and stimulating group of students with primary interest in the humanities.

Heterogeneity among the students should be achieved as far as practical. To be sure that the College is realistic in its mix in terms of the normal University clientele it should purposely devise some means of giving equal opportunity to Florida students from the rural areas as well as from the urban centers. Both men and women will be equally acceptable for admission.

Students will be given quickly to understand that they will be assigned heavy responsibilities, not only for self-management but also for the basic operations of the College itself. They will be given responsibilities along with the faculty in curriculum, administration, fiscal matters, physical surroundings, social and other activities, and evaluation of the College's achievements. In relation to the professors, students will be looked upon as partners in learning, albeit junior partners.

It will be the responsibility of the students as well as the faculty to create a climate in which intellectual pursuits can be carried on with the least amount of obstruction. It is easy to envision a Utopia for the College in which students when they are not in class are busy painting pictures, singing in choral groups, playing chamber music, absorbed in good books, or reading love poems to each other. While no such Utopia is possible or even desirable, it ought to be made easy for any student to read, write, or paint without feeling he is hopelessly out of joint with his fellow students.

The "well-behaved" student is not necessarily the most acceptable one. We do not wish for him the awful fate of being constantly happy or well adjusted. We will prize him because he is unhappy about many things and wishes to correct them. We will value him because he is able to think critically. But this capacity will be encouraged in him not to cause him to lapse in colorless objectivity or frustrating doubt, but that he may achieve inward poise and a workable faith.

A student will be accepted and allowed to remain in the College on the premise that his basic loyalty is to the College. He should be encouraged to participate in University events which stretch his imagination or increase his skills. When such outside participation infringes on his loyalty to the College, it is doubtful whether his own best ends can be served by the College. Surely the College should deny to itself the role of "adolescent reservation" to use David Boroff's expressive phrase. The student must not be fenced off from serious adult concerns. But if he becomes so overly absorbed with some of these—such as race relations, politics, religion, sex, or intercollegiate athletics—he may find his concerns as a student thereby diminished.

Since we have emphasized the maturing of the student during his college life, surely we should expect a measure of maturity before we put our stamp of approval on him. It would be a grim jest to call his education completed. It should only be the beginning. He should demonstrate that he has walked as a contemporary with the great men and ideas of the past and gotten a faint glimmer of the grandeur of which the human spirit is capable. Having conversed with Socrates, sailed with Columbus, and seen Hamlet at the Globe, something surely measurable must have happened to him.

The Library

The library will be a focal point of learning in the College. Living with books and teaching with books will be basic operating procedures. As already mentioned, every professional person connected with the College is expected to be first and primarily a teacher. This is doubly true of the professional librarians. Their approach in working with students must always be that of a teacher.

It should be impossible for any student to graduate from the College without a genuine knowledge of and interest in books. It will be our aim to send the graduate out into the world with a realization that his education is just beginning and that the enrichment of his life and the contribution he will make to society will depend in no small measure on the books that become his lifetime companions.

If we are to achieve such a result, students must have access to books at all times in the library, dormitory, and classrooms.

We shall develop the College's library collection with the intent of having sufficient copies of all the standard works of well-known authors the world over, not just of the Western world. Many of these books will need to be in the original language as well as in English. While major works of reference, such as dictionaries in various languages and the major encyclopedias, should be readily accessible, no attempt will be made to duplicate the much more comprehensive reference collections available in the University library. Nor need the College library include books of the kind that, because of their inherent value or the difficulty of replacement, are normally kept on reserve or in the rare book and special collections departments of the University library. This is not to say that such books will have no place in the lives of the students. On the contrary, students will be encouraged to make use of these special collections and their research projects will frequently call for their examination of such materials. It should be the responsibility of the University library staff and the Library School to instruct the new student in the content and the use of these resources of the University. Students should have ready access to certain current magazines, of course, but for the most part these will be found in the University library.

The College library will also have art reproductions, musical recordings, and slides available for students to use in connection with their reading.

The students will be encouraged to own books and to build up personal libraries.

In physical planning it is most important that the library be in the center of activities, flexible, comfortable, appealing, and without distractions. It should at all times be a laboratory for the use of books, easily adaptable to change. Perhaps the book shelves should be located in a large open area flanked by many alcoves and classrooms.

There will be no barriers between the student and the books. In the educational process a book in the hand in worth twenty on the shelf. The open-shelf policy is essential and the checking-out and return process will be as simple and free from restrictions as possible.

The books will be cataloged on computer tape, making it possible to print as many complete or partial lists of the collection as are needed. There will be an inexpensive copying service at a point near the books.

If we agree that a book in the hand is worth twenty on the shelf, we would probably also agree that a book on display is worth ten on a shelf. All types of books will be liberally displayed, and the holdings of the rare book room and special collections of the University library by this means will be kept before the students on a continuing and rotating basis.

The Facilities of the College

Based on his training at Oxford, Cardinal Newman in his *Idea of the University* written over a hundred years ago urged the educational value of a proper living environment for college students: "They get for themselves new ideas and new views, fresh matter for thought, and distinct principles for judging and acting day by day." American universities, dominated by the German university concept, have been less willing to give as much educational significance to halls of residence as might have been the case had the English university viewpoint prevailed. Within the last decade, however, there has been renewed interest in residence halls as fruitful places of learning. The College hopes to incorporate the educational advantages of the English halls of residence.

There will be at least four dormitory wings attached to a central social, academic, and functional core. Each residence hall will accommodate no more than 100 students. Some of the rooms in each unit will be single rooms. Both single rooms and double rooms will be clustered in units of eight to twelve students sharing common bath facilities and study area. Each hall will have no more than four floors, preferably less. The first floor will contain a laundry. The first floor of the building housing women will also have a large hobby room containing equipment and materials of peculiar interest to women such as sewing machines and dress models. There will be a small kitchen for trying their culinary skills on their friends. The hobby area in the dormitory for men will include such things as vises, drills, saws, and an assortment of tools.

Colorful simplicity will be reflected both in the architecture and in the interior decorations of all buildings. Materials such as cinder-block walls and carpeted floors not only will reduce building costs but will add color and coziness as well. The "institutional look" will be minimized and the characteristics of home enhanced by architectural styling and arrangement. There will be many places for informal and relaxed lounging. A most important consideration and one which will receive maximum attention from the designer is reduction of noise and reverberations.

The auditorium will be large enough to seat all the students and faculty of the College. It will be used by faculty lecturers, visiting lecturers, and also as a place for presenting plays, skits, debates, and programs of chamber music. For this reason the auditorium will have a stage and two dressing rooms. The kiva design of Michigan State University offers interesting possibilities. There will be four teaching classrooms seating about 100 students each. Each of these will be equipped with certain mechanical devices, like visual aids, as adjuncts to lectures or demonstrations. One of these will be equipped as a science lecture room capable of giving basic demonstrations in the physical and biological sciences. However, each room will double in the evening as a social area. This means that the architect must arrange for maximum flexibility, possibly with movable walls to permit the accommodation of large or small groups as occasion requires.

There will be about 10 small seminar-lounge rooms, none seating more than 25 and most seating only 10 or 15 persons. Since it is assumed that the dialectic method of teaching will generally prevail, the rooms will be furnished and arranged so as to stimulate good conversation. Each of these rooms will be equipped with programed instructional materials of the type that encourage individual initiative. Since one such instrument is a small phonograph for language instruction, these rooms will all double as music listening rooms or social rooms in the evening. A game of bridge or of chess or a lively conversation will frequently follow the instructional activities of the day.

Perhaps there will be a small room equipped for prayer and meditation. This could become a place of sentiment, of happy memories, of whispered griefs, of inner strengthening.

There will be a few professors' apartments of two bedrooms each. In addition to a living room, dining room and kitchen area, each apartment will have a study serving not only as the professor's office but for his seminar room as well.

Conclusion

We confess that in all of these proposals there is nothing which has not been tried somewhere and at some time. Are we then trying to turn back the hands of the clock to the "good old days"? American higher education owes much to a rich heritage of principles, traditions, and techniques handed down from ancient Greece and Alexandria, from medieval centers of learning, and from universities in England and on the Continent. For instance, we propose using conversation between students and teachers as a fundamental teaching technique. This is not new, of course, because many centuries ago Plato had already concluded as he wrote in a fragment called the "Seventh Flag" that "there is no learning without dialectic." The preacher can then mock us that ours is just another vanity.

Lo, this is new?
It was already in existence in the Ages
Which were before us.

But Marjorie Carpenter, quoting Paul Tillich, has helped us establish a philosophical justification for labeling our proposals a "new kind of college." In times when pressures force us to perpetuate some of the less desirable features of higher education—large classes, heavy reliance on lectures, growing emphasis on research at the expense of teaching, impersonalization —we believe that we are turning back to the eternal qualities which, because they are eternal, are also new.

If these ideas can be combined into a program that provides

a better education for the student, it matters little whether the ideas are new or centuries old. The basic test will be the end product—a student well equipped and well motivated for a lifelong career of learning.

Chapter 13

BEHOLD, YOU HAVE CREATED A NEW THING: SUMMARY AND CRITIQUE

By B. Lamar Johnson*

In selecting the title for this presentation from the closing paragraph of the opening address of the conference I have no thought of suggesting that a complacent self-satisfaction has been characteristic of this colloquium. Quite the contrary. If anything has marked this conference it has been the presence of a spirit of what might be designated "divine discontent."

Our deliberations these past three days have served to reinforce the words of President Blackwell when, in his opening statement of welcome, he uttered what was proved to be the understatement of the conference: "All is not well with undergraduate education." Indeed, in a sense, this conference might be epitomized by the assertion: "All is not well with undergraduate education in our experimental colleges."

What I am saying was well stated by a member of this colloquium as he and I made our way to the dining room for the opening dinner of the conference. "Our major problem," he explained, "is that we know too much about ourselves."

The title I have chosen represents an ideal toward which the experimental college is pressing. "Is the clue then," asks Miss Carpenter in the opening address of the conference, "to a genuinely experimental college a faculty which can be fired with the idea of passionately striving for the new? . . . . Is the key for the administration, now pathetically bogged down with financial worries, a shift to this same passionate striving for the new?"

Please do not misunderstand me. This conference has not

---

*Mr. Johnson is Professor of Higher Education, University of California, Los Angeles, California.

suggested "new simply for the sake of being new." It has, however, urged the new for the sake of better achieving accepted purposes.

Let us not, this conference boldly proclaims, concentrate on patches! Let us create a new thing! Or, as we contemplate the diversity of colleges here represented, we might better clarion: Let us create new things!

Each of us has come to Wakulla Springs with different backgrounds and concerns, different hopes and aspirations. Your perceptions of what has happened during the .past three days will in all likelihood vary from mine. Accordingly as I relate my impression of the colloquium I suggest that you check them against your own.

I propose to report my impressions under four headings:

1. This is our definition of the experimental college.

2. These are trends in experimental colleges.

3. These are realities we have neglected or minimized.

4. These are problems in experimental colleges.

As I report my observations, please remember that this presentation is based upon the papers and discussions of the past three days. I am presenting possible national thinking and trends only to the extent that the colleges participating in this colloquium are representative of those across the country. As I refer to colleges or experimental colleges I am then speaking only of those institutions represented here.

Definition

It has been refreshing to attend a conference during which major attention has not been given to definition of terms. We have come here to exchange views, experiences, and findings regarding experimental colleges—and also to share our aspirations and dreams. And we have done just this. Without preliminary sparring—dotting *i*'s and crossing *t*'s—we moved immediately to the tasks and opportunities that were at hand.

The closest that we came to a definition of the experimental college was in Miss Carpenter's address when she explained, "Very simply, this is an educational institution which is trying to be a college."

We at this colloquium have known what we have in mind. Why split hairs on definitions? I am reminded of the sage comment of one of our leading exponents of jazz: "Man, if you have to ask what jazz is, you'll never get to know."

Trends

As we have engaged in dialogue these past three days, it has appeared to me that there have been reported fifteen trends or developments which characterize the experimental colleges:

1. The colleges represented at this conference tend either to have relatively small enrollments or to be divided into manageably small units. The emergence of separate experimental entities within large institutions has impressed me as much as any single development reported. I refer to the colleges at the University of the Pacific and at the University of California at Santa Cruz, to Monteith College of Wayne State University, to the residence hall plan of Michigan State University and to the house plan at Stephens College—not to mention the experimental college plan under study at Florida State University. Repeatedly it has been suggested these past three days that separate colleges—or other units—can form a basis for innovating developments, even within a large and complex university. In the words of a slogan at the University of the Pacific, "We grow larger by becoming smaller"—a concept which is echoed at the University of California at Santa Cruz, where the goal is "to seem smaller as it grows larger."

2. Most of the colleges represented at this conference are young institutions. Let me call the roll of these: New College, the Dearborn Campus of the University of Michigan, Florida Presbyterian College, Monteith College, the University of California at Santa Cruz, and the new colleges of the University of the Pacific. I call your attention, however, to the fact that some of our colleges—Antioch and Stephens, for example—have been "in the business" for several decades.

3. Eight of the 10 colleges whose programs have been reported are residential institutions. Only Monteith College and the Dearborn Campus of the University of Michigan are commuting institutions. And the Dearborn campus is soon to have some residence halls. Projections under consideration at the

Florida State University are also centered around residential units.

4. The experimental colleges participating in this colloquium tend to emphasize the liberal arts or general education. Only the Dearborn Campus of the University of Michigan frankly highlights technology and preparation for earning a livelihood—along with a recognition of the liberal arts. In the words of Dr. Stirton, "The Dearborn Campus program is not an 'either . . . or'; rather it represents a *both . . . and* ' approach to *both* the liberal arts *and* to technology and preparation for earning a livelihood."

5. With a single exception—the Dearborn Campus of the University of Michigan—the colleges participating in this conference have four-year programs. The Dearborn Campus—which is located adjacent to Henry Ford Community College—has offerings for the junior and senior years and for graduate work.

6. The colleges at this colloquium have selective admission policies. All (except Parsons College) have admission requirements based upon such factors as high school grades, aptitude tests, and achievement tests. Factors of economic selection also operate for most and perhaps all of the colleges.

7. Experimental colleges emphasize independent study, both as a means of learning and as a goal of education. It is notable that independent study is planned and used for all—not simply for honor students. Our discussions of this development have included such phrases as "responsibility of students," and "faith in students." Representative of institutions which particularly stress independent study are Antioch College, Florida Presbyterian College, and New College.

8. The programs of the colleges tend to be student-centered. During our days together we have considered such varying concepts as content-centered, library-centered, faculty-centered—as well as student-centered programs; and yet we have repeatedly returned to the individual student as the central entity in the experimental college. Flexibility and individualization of both content and rate of learning are commonly reported.

As I have listened to the discussions of these past three days, however, I have not been able to erase from my memory the sage comments of a skeptical colleague of mine who, in referring to colleges' offerings asserts: "They are not student-centered; nor are they content- or library-centered. College instruction is essentially grade-centered, with students aiming to determine what 'the old buzzard' wants and then giving it to him. The student gets the grades that he wants and needs—and that is his goal." This view in which there is, I fear, more truth than fiction leads to the statement of another characteristic of the experimental college.

9. The experimental college stresses the importance of evaluation in appraising both the achievement of individual students and the effectiveness of the educational program—in whole or in part. Noted during the conference has been, for example, the work of the professional assessor at New College. Also notable are the responsibilities of the Director of Program Development and Research at Antioch College and the Director of Institutional Research at Michigan State University. Despite the emphasis on evaluation in experimental colleges we have, during the past three days, heard some evidence of an almost evangelistic commitment to and enthusiasm for programs—apparently untempered by judicial appraisal.

10. The library occupies a position of special importance in the experimental college. Many and varied are the plans and suggestions made for libraries during these three days: special college and house libraries; completely open shelves and ready access to books 24 hours a day; the library as a center of varied resources of learning—including not only books and other printed matter but also audio-visual materials; the provision of carrels or offices for independent study by students; the use of the library—in totality, if you will—as the textbook for teaching; the development and use of systematic library assignments for purposes of substantive teaching and also to provide a thorough and comprehensive grounding in the process of using the library as a tool for learning (as at Monteith College); the fusion of the library and the teaching faculty into a single instructional staff—epitomized perhaps by the observation that the classroom flows into the library and the library flows into the classrooms.

Varied are the plans that are used or contemplated. Unanimous agreement is reached, however, on the assertion that the library can and must have a notable role in the experimental college, a role based upon the particular goals, organization, and program of a given institution.

11. Experimental colleges select faculty members with particular care. Flexibility and commitment are the requirements for faculty members most emphasized during our colloquium.

12. There is a trend in some colleges toward expecting students to pay the entire cost of their education. When this policy is followed, generous fellowships are sought. In the words of one administrator, "We will accept the rich and able and will take care of the able."

13. Experimental colleges tend to have all-year sessions. The use of three terms—sometimes designated as trimesters—appears to be the plan most frequently followed.

14. Among experimental colleges there is much discussion about eliminating grades and credits. Actually, however, comparatively few advances appear to have been made in this direction. Grades have, upon occasion, been simplified or extended over lengthy periods in the student's program. Also advances have been made in granting credit by examination.

15. The experimental college is—and most would hold must be—in a constant state of flux and change. The very commitment to students which we have stressed makes flexibility necessary. For, we have noted, students change as indeed the world changes. Also we modify our programs as we evaluate what we are doing on the basis of our purposes. Change again is inevitable.

Change has been termed the only certainty in life. Change is, it would seem, doubly certain in the experimental college.

Neglected Realities

It is impossible within a three day period to be all things to all men—even within the restricted world of the experimental colleges. It has obviously been necessary to limit our agenda. Nevertheless, there are a number of realities in American life and education which condition the function, the operation, and the influence of the experimental college. I should like to refer to nine of these realities which we have neglected or to which we have given minimal attention.

1. Managerial problems. The conference committee is to be congratulated in omitting from our agenda matters of managerial operation which typically occupy so much of our time and attention at conferences. Our publics—alumni, donors, legislators; square and cubic footage; indices of space utilization; budgets and balance sheets—these are all important in the functioning of the experimental college. Nevertheless, I am pleased that during this colloquium we have found it possible to give major attention to curriculum and program.

2. The commuting college. The commuting college and university must increasingly be recognized as an emerging pattern for much—and I venture to assert most—of American higher education. The student lives at home. He comes to campus for his classes and for some of his studying. We may bewail this situation—but it is a reality. For millions of youth the choice is and will be a commuting college—or no college at all. This is a reality which we have neglected—or at best minimized—these past three days.

3. Programed learning. There is an undeniable ferment of programed learning in American education. At times I fear that programed instruction is unthinkingly accepted and adopted as a fad. It is perfectly clear, therefore, that much of what is currently done is superficial and endangers a development which has much to offer American education. In particular, programed learning would appear to offer promise to the experimental college which is committed to individualization. Programed learning has been minimized in our discussions of the past three days.

4. Technological aids to teaching. In an age of technology, education has an opportunity to use aids to teaching and learning that were unknown and even undreamed of a generation ago. Television—open and closed circuit—and electronic facilities for listening and viewing are representative developments which give every reason for examining and re-examining the organization and processes of college teaching. Technological aids to learning may permit economies in teaching (including

large group instruction in appropriate situations) which will make possible—in other situations—individualized and personalized teaching—"eyeball to eyeball confrontation," if you will. It has also been suggested here that such developments as television may result in decentralized—and some would suggest distintegrated—campuses. What might this mean for the experimental college? We have here given only minimal consideration to television and other technological aids to learning.

5. Technology and preparation for earning a livelihood. We are living in an age of science and technology and in a society in which man is called upon to earn a livelihood. In our deliberations we have given minimal consideration to technology in the curriculum and to the reality of student motivations to prepare themselves for employment.

6. Clearer definition of purposes. Obviously the curriculum of a college—and in particular that of an experimental college—must be based upon a clear definition of purposes. We have a diversity of colleges and universities: large and small, public and private, rural and urban, commuting and residential, selective and open door, liberal and specialized. Our nation has a need for varied types of institutions with a diversity of purposes. But there is one type of institution which we do not require. I refer to the college which has failed specifically to define its purposes—or having defined them, fails to design its program to achieve its goals. I have in mind, for example, the college whose intellectual objectives are belied by its emphasis on big time football; or to the college which aims to foster independence of thought and action—and yet uses a rigidly scheduled program of lectures, followed by regurgitating examinations. At Wakulla Springs we have given minimal attention to the clear definition of purposes and the development of programs which directly emerge from these goals.

7. Findings of research. In general, this conference has not been research oriented. We have had few reports of studies which evaluate the effectiveness of the experimental college. We talk in general terms about research and experimentation. But in reality we tend to neglect these activities. Perhaps, as has been suggested, we should use the term "innovating college," rather than "experimental college."

8. The two-year college. One out of every four students entering college attends a junior college. More than three-fourths of the freshmen and sophomores in California institutions of higher education are in junior colleges. We are meeting in the state in which many would say the junior college has had its most notable development during the past five years. We are in the early months of a year during which both the Educational Policies Commission and Secretary of Labor Wirtz have urged the upward extension of free public education through the sophomore year of college.

Alvin C. Eurich, in an article in the June, 1963, issue of the *Atlantic Monthly* entitled "Higher Education in the 21st Century," predicts that by the year 2000 many strong liberal arts colleges and universities will have discontinued their first two undergraduate years since the responsibility for lower-division education will have come "almost wholly within the province of the junior college."

The trend is clear: junior colleges will increasingly assume responsibility for preparing students to enter the junior year of senior institutions. And yet these past three days we have been discussing experimental colleges almost entirely within the context of an assumed continuing four-year period in a single institution. We have neglected the reality of the two-year college.

9. Implications of the experimental college for American higher education. The significance of experimental colleges rests only in part on the effect they have on the lives and thinking of those students who attend them. Only a tiny percentage of the college students of our nation attend or will attend experimental colleges. The importance of these colleges must extend far beyond their alumni. The experimental college has an opportunity and indeed an obligation to influence and take leadership in the mainstream of American higher education. This is, however, a responsibility which we have largely neglected in the past three days. I am particularly concerned with this neglect when I contemplate the minimal attention we have given to the realities, for example, of both the commuting college and the two-year college. The influence and leadership of the experimental college will inevitably be restricted if it re-

mains separated from the reality of the mainstream of American higher education.

Problems

A formerly popular television program—or is it still in vogue?—was introduced by the announcement, "We have letters." I paraphrase this pronouncement as I introduce the final section of this presentation: "We have problems." Of many which might be discussed I have chosen to comment on four.

1. The conflict between research and teaching. In essence the experimental college is faced with the necessity of developing a program which meets both the needs of students and the requirements of a faculty. A corollary to this problem has been suggested during this conference: "As graduate programs develop, undergraduate programs suffer."

Although there have been few expressions of this view here, some would hold that carrying on research is essential to teaching of the highest order. Others would insist that there must be opportunity for research for those faculty members who wish to engage in this type of activity. Still others would point to research as necessary for promotion at their institutions. The University of California at Santa Cruz—an institution in which research is essential to promotion—proposes to face this problem by having joint assignments to the teaching facilities of small colleges and to the scholarly pursuits of departmental disciplines. Monteith College on the contrary meets this issue by appointing staff members to full-time instructional positions and by providing stimuli to creativity through teaching.

It is clear that in the academic market place research is at present the currency of the realm. The scholar who achieves distinction in teaching without a similar distinction in research is at a distinct disadvantage in academic bartering. The experimental college must, therefore, either provide an opportunity and stimulus for research, along with teaching, or it must provide emoluments for faculty members which are comparable with those received by distinguished research scholars. If the experimental college fails in this, it will either be unable to build and maintain a superior faculty or it will be asking its staff members and their families in fact to subsidize the costs of education as they make unjustifiable financial sacrifices.

2. Finance. We have given comparatively little direct attention to financing experimental colleges. And yet the specter of reality has been constantly before us. Some colleges frankly acknowledge that their costs are and must be high. They seek and secure funds to finance costly programs. Other institutions plan offerings within a budget which is consistent with those of other colleges within their states—or perhaps within their own institutions. The problem of finance must ever be before us in education. This is particularly and uniquely true in the experimental college.

3. "Take over." Because of the nature of their programs and because of their possible implications for other segments of higher education, experimental colleges frequently secure grants from foundations or other donors. Such gifts are often used to pay the costs of new ventures. But inevitably, there comes the time that the grant expires and a decision must be made: can we "take over" and continue the program which has been paid for by a grant? Or must we drop it for want of funds?

The history of American higher education is replete with examples of "successful experiments" which have been discontinued. During the past three days we have heard examples of the "take over" and continuation of successful innovations. At Monteith College, for example, we are told of a library experiment which has proved its values and for which plans for "take over" are well advanced.

When "take over" is neglected the experimental college is failing to meet one of its responsibilities.

4. I have postponed to the last a problem which has loomed particularly large these past three days. I am referring to the difficulty of maintaining a sense of urgency and adventure and a zest for change in a long-established and "successful program." Most of the colleges here represented are relatively new. Theirs is the good fortune to be in a period of pioneering enthusiasm and yet even these young colleges are becoming aware of the potential dangers of maturity and old age. Witness New College and its resolution to retain—permanently, it is sug-

gested—the name New College. The purpose is to epitomize the character of an institution committed to change.

In considering this problem I would like, first briefly to refer to leadership and finally to make a recommendation.

In a chapter in a volume published earlier this year, *Behavioral Science and Educational Administration*,[1] James M. Lipham of the University of Wisconsin suggests a dilemma as he proposes a distinction between leadership and administration.

> We may define leadership as the initiation of a new structure or procedure for accomplishing an organization's goals and objectives or for changing an organization's goals and objectives. Note that the emphasis here is upon initiating change . . . . the leader is concerned with initiating changes in established structures, procedures, or goals; he is disruptive of the existing state of affairs.
>
> The administrator, on the other hand, may be identified as the individual who utilizes existing structures or procedures to achieve an organizational goal or objective . . . . the administrator is concerned primarily with maintaining rather than changing, established structures, procedures, or goals. Thus the administrator may be viewed as a stabilizing force.
>
> In view of the foregoing distinction between administration and leadership, it becomes apparent that the oft-used term "administrative leadership" is something of a paradox. To characterize a given behavioral act as "administrative leadership" is to fail to recognize a source of conflict . . . between the administrative role and the leadership role.[2]

I paraphrase Professor Lipham as I suggest that a college president must at times wear an "administrative hat" and at other times a "leadership hat." Having but one head, the president should be aware of which hat he is wearing—since he is clearly expected both to administer and to lead.

The dilemma which the president faces is accentuated if he is the chief administrator of an experimental college. Here,

[1]*Behavioral Science and Educational Administration.* The sixty-third yearbook of the National Society for the Study of Education. Part II. University of Chicago Press, 1964.

[2]*Ibid.* pp. 122-123.

indeed, leadership is essential—for the experimental college is committed to creating the new.

With this in mind I would like to make a suggestion to experimental colleges. This proposal in a somewhat different context was advanced by Philip Coombs in an address at UCLA.[3] My suggestion—in fact my urgent recommendation—is that every experimental college appoint a Vice President in Charge of Heresy. No administrative responsibility is attached to this post. It is a leadership position. Our Vice President is expected to be a dreamer. He will attend meetings such as this and in particular assemble the "far out" proposals. He will needle his faculty colleagues and will in turn be needled by them. He will study the findings of research and analyze their implications for this college.

He will, in short, be a harbinger of change. Why not a Vice President in Charge of Heresy at each of our experimental colleges? And, who knows, we might soon have a national conference and organization of vice presidents in charge of heresy!

Conclusion

These past few days we have been on a quest—a quest for the new and the promising. We have viewed with alarm and we have shared with alacrity. We have turned to the past but in particular we have faced the future.

Regardless of whether we may be surveying trends in the experimental college, identifying realities we have neglected, or examining problems which confront us, we must recognize the truth of the assertion which comes to each of us: "Behold, you have created a new thing." Let us keep it new for "It is not the old which creates the new. That which creates the new is beyond the old and beyond the new."

[3]Philip H. Coombs. *The Technical Frontiers of Education*. The twenty-seventh annual Sir John Adams Lecture at the University of California, Los Angeles . . . . March 15, 1960 (School of Education, University of California, Los Angeles, 1960). pp. 14-15.